D0726892

A GUIDE TO
KING LEAR

SHAUN McCARTHY

WITH TONY BUZAN

Hodder & Stoughton

ISBN 0 340 77562 9

First published 2000
Impression number   10 9 8   7 6 5 4 3 2 1
Year   2005   2004 2003 2002 2001 2000

Cover photograph: © David Cooper – Photostage
Illustrations: David Ashby
Mind Maps: Anne Jones – Buzan Centres Ltd.

Typeset by Transet Limited, Coventry, England.
Printed in Great Britain for Hodder & Stoughton Educational, a division of
Hodder Headline Plc, 338 Euston Road, London NW1 3BH by Cox and Wyman Ltd,
Reading, Berks.

ONTENTS

You are now in the most important educational stage of your life, and are soon to take English Literature exams that may have a major impact on your future career and goals. As one A-level student put it: 'It's crunch time!'

At this crucial stage of your life the one thing you need even more than subject knowledge is the knowledge of *how* to remember, *how* to read faster, *how* to comprehend, *how* to study, *how* to take notes and *how* to organize your thoughts. You need to know how to *think*; you need a basic introduction on how to use that super bio-computer inside your head – your brain.

The next eight pages contain a goldmine of information on how you can achieve success both at school and in your A-level English literature exams, as well as in your professional or university career. These eight pages will give you skills that will enable you to be successful in *all* your academic pursuits. You will learn:

◆ How to recall more *while* you are learning.
◆ How to recall more *after* you have finished a class or a study period.
◆ How to use special techniques to improve your memory.
◆ How to use a revolutionary note-taking technique called Mind Maps that will double your memory and help you to write essays and answer exam questions.
◆ How to read everything faster while at the same time improving your comprehension and concentration.
◆ How to zap your revision!

How to understand, improve and master your memory of Literature Guides

Your memory really is like a muscle. Don't exercise it and it will grow weaker; *do* exercise it properly and it will grow incredibly more powerful. There are really only four main things you need to understand about your memory in order to increase its power dramatically:

Recall during learning
– YOU MUST TAKE BREAKS!

When you are studying, your memory can concentrate, understand and recall well for between 20 and 45 minutes at a time. Then it *needs* a break. If you carry on for longer than this without one, your memory starts to break down. If you study for hours non-stop, you will remember only a fraction of what you have been trying to learn, and you will have wasted valuable revision time.

So, ideally, *study for less than an hour*, then take a five- to ten-minute break. During this break listen to music, go for a walk, do some exercise, or just daydream. (Daydreaming is a necessary brain-power booster – geniuses do it regularly.) During the break your brain will be sorting out what it has been learning and you will go back to your study with the new information safely stored and organized in your memory banks. Make *sure* you take breaks at regular intervals as you work through the *Literature Guides*.

Recall after learning
– SURFING THE WAVES OF YOUR MEMORY

What do you think begins to happen to your memory straight *after* you have finished learning something? Does it immediately start forgetting? No! Surprisingly, your brain actually *increases* its power and carries on remembering. For a short time after your study session, your brain integrates the information, making a more complete picture of everything it has just learnt. Only then does the rapid decline in memory begin, as much as 80 per cent of what you have learnt can be forgotten in a day.

However, if you catch the top of the wave of your memory, and briefly review what you have been revising at the correct time, the memory is stamped in far more strongly, and stays at the crest of the wave for a much longer time. To maximize your brain's power to remember, take a few minutes and use a Mind Map to review what you have learnt at the end of a day. Then review it at the end of a week, again at the end of a month, and finally a week before the exams. That way you'll surf-ride your memory wave all the way to your exam, success and beyond!

The memory principle of association

The muscle of your memory becomes stronger when it can **associate** – when it can link things together.

Think about your best friend, and all the things your mind *automatically* links with that person. Think about your favourite hobby, and all the associations your mind has when you think about (remember!) that hobby.

When you are studying, use this memory principle to make associations between the elements in your subjects, and thus to improve both your memory and your chances of success.

The memory principle of imagination

The muscle of your memory will improve significantly if you can produce big images in your mind. Rather than just memorizing the name of a character, imagine that character of the novel or play as if you were a video producer filming that person's life. The same goes for images in poetry.

In *all* your subjects use the **imagination** memory principle.

Throughout this *Literature Guide* you will find special association and imagination techniques (called mnemonics after the Greek goddess Mnemosyne) that will make it much easier for you to remember the topic being discussed. Look out for them!

Your new success formula: Mind Maps®

You have noticed that when people go on holidays, or travel, they take maps. Why? To give them a general picture of where they are going, to help them locate places of special interest and importance, to help them find things more easily, and to help them remember distances and locations, etc.

It is exactly the same with your mind and with study. If you have a 'map of the territory' of what you have to learn, then everything is easier. In learning and study, the Mind Map is that special tool.

As well as helping you with all areas of study, the Mind Map actually *mirrors the way your brain works.* Your Mind Maps can be used for taking notes from your study books, for taking notes in class, for preparing your homework, for presenting your homework, for reviewing your tests, for checking your and your friends' knowledge in any subject, and for *helping you understand anything you learn.* Mind Maps are especially useful in English literature, as they allow you to map out the whole territory of a novel, play or poem, giving you an 'at-a-glance' snapshot of all the key information you need to know.

The Mind Maps in the *Literature Guide* use, throughout, **imagination** and **association**. As such, they automatically strengthen your memory muscle every time you use them. Throughout this guide you will find Mind Maps that summarize the most important areas of the English Literature guide you are studying. Study these Mind Maps, add some colour, personalize them, and then have a go at making your own Mind Maps of the work you are studying – you will remember them far better! Put them on your walls and in your files for a quick and easy review. Mind Maps are fast, efficient, effective and, importantly, *fun* to do!

HOW TO DRAW A MIND MAP

1 Start in the middle of the page with the page turned sideways. This gives your brain more radiant freedom for its thoughts.

2 Always start by drawing a picture or symbol of the novel or its title. Why? Because *a picture is worth a thousand words to your brain.* Try to use at least three colours, as colour helps your memory even more.

3 Let your thoughts flow, and write or draw your ideas on coloured branching lines connected to your central image. The key symbols and words are the headings for your topic. The Mind Map at the top of the next page shows you how to start.

4 Next, add facts and ideas by drawing more, smaller, branches on to the appropriate main branches, just like a tree.

5 Always print your word clearly on its line. Use only one word per line.

6 To link ideas and thoughts on different branches, use arrows, colours, underlining and boxes.

HOW TO READ A MIND MAP

1 Begin in the centre, the focus of your novel, play or poem.

2 The words/images attached to the centre are like chapter headings; read them next.

3 Always read out from the centre, in every direction (even on the left-hand side, where you will read from right to left, instead of the usual left to right).

USING MIND MAPS

Mind Maps are a versatile tool – use them for taking notes in class or from books, for solving problems, for brainstorming with friends, and for reviewing and revising for exams – their uses are infinite! You will find them invaluable for planning essays for coursework and exams. Number your main branches in the order in which you want to use them and off you go – the main headings for your essay are done and all your ideas are logically organized!

Super speed reading and study

What do you think happens to your comprehension as your reading speed rises? 'It goes down!' Wrong! It seems incredible, but it has been proved – the faster you read, the more you comprehend and remember!

So here are some tips to help you to practise reading faster – you'll cover the ground much more quickly, remember more, *and* have more time for revision and leisure activities!

SUPER SPEED READING

1 First read the whole text (whether it's a lengthy book or an exam paper) very quickly, to give your brain an overall idea of what's ahead and get it working.
(It's like sending out a scout to look at the territory you have to cover – it's much easier when you know what to expect!) Then read the text again for more detailed information.
2 Have the text a reasonable distance away from your eyes. In this way your eye/brain system will be able to see more at a glance, and will naturally begin to read faster.
3 Take in groups of words at a time. Rather than reading 'slowly and carefully' read faster, more enthusiastically. Your comprehension will rocket!
4 Take in phrases rather than single words while you read.
5 Use a guide. Your eyes are designed to follow movement, so a thin pencil underneath the lines you are reading, moved smoothly along, will 'pull' your eyes to faster speeds.

HOW TO MAKE STUDY EASY FOR YOUR BRAIN

When you are going somewhere, is it easier to know beforehand where you are going, or not? Obviously it is easier if you *do* know. It is the same for your brain and a book. When you get a new book, there are seven things you can do to help your brain get to 'know the territory' faster:

1 Scan through the whole book in less than 20 minutes, as you would do if you were in a shop thinking whether or not to buy it. This gives your brain *control*.

2 Think about what you already know about the subject. You'll often find out it's a lot more than you thought. A good way of doing this is to do a quick Mind Map on *everything you know* after you have skimmed through it.

3 Ask who, what, why, where, when and how questions about what is in the book. Questions help your brain 'fish' the knowledge out.

4 Ask your friends what they know about the subject. This helps them review the knowledge in their own brains, and helps your brain get new knowledge about what you are studying.

5 Have another quick speed read through the book, this time looking for any diagrams, pictures and illustrations, and also at the beginnings and ends of chapters. Most information is contained in the beginnings and ends.

6 If you come across any difficult parts in your book, mark them and *move on*. Your brain *will* be able to solve the problems when you come back to them a bit later. Much like saving the difficult bits of a jigsaw puzzle for later. When you have finished the book, quickly review it one more time and then discuss it with friends. This will lodge it permanently in your memory banks.

7 Build up a Mind Map as you study the book. This helps your brain to organize and hold (remember!) information as you study.

Helpful hints for exam revision

◆ To avoid **exam panic** cram at the *start* of your course, not the end. It takes the same amount of time, so you may as well use it where it is best placed!

◆ Use Mind Maps throughout your course, and build a Master Mind Map for each subject – a giant Mind Map that summarizes everything you know about the subject.

◆ Use memory techniques such as mnemonics (verses or systems for remembering things like dates and events or lists).

◆ Get together with one or two friends to revise, compare Mind Maps, and discuss topics.

AND FINALLY ...

◆ *Have fun while you learn* – studies show that those people who enjoy what they are doing understand and remember it more, and generally do better.

◆ *Use your teachers* as resource centres. Ask them for help with specific topics and with more general advice on how you can improve your all-round performance.

◆ *Personalize your* **Literature Revision Guide** *by underlining and highlighting, by adding notes and pictures. Allow your brain to have a conversation with it!*

Your amazing brain and its amazing cells

Your brain is like a super, *super, SUPER* computer. The world's best computers have only a few thousand or hundred thousand computer chips. Your brain has 'computer chips' too, and they are called brain cells. Unlike the computer, you do not have only a few thousand computer chips – the number of brain cells in your head is a *million MILLION*!! This means you are a genius just waiting to discover yourself! All you have to do is learn how to get those brain cells working together, and you'll not only become more smart, you'll have more free time to pursue your other fun activities.

The more you understand your amazing brain the more it will repay and amaze you!

Apply its power to this *Literature Guide*!

(Tony Buzan)

HOW TO USE THIS GUIDE

This guide assumes that you have already read *King Lear,* although you could read 'Context' and 'The story of *King Lear'* first. It is best to use the guide alongside the play. You could read the 'Characterization' and 'Themes' sections without referring to it, but you will get more out of these if you do.

The sections

The 'Commentary' section can be used in a number of ways. One way is to read a scene of the play, and then read the relevant commentary. Keep on until you come to a test section, test yourself – then have a break! Alternatively, read the Commentary for a scene, then read that scene in the play, then go back to the Commentary. See what works best for you.

'Critical approaches' sums up the main critical views and interpretations of the play. Your own response is important, but be aware of these approaches too.

'How to get an "A" in English Literature' gives valuable advice on what to look for in a text, and what skills you need to develop in order to achieve your personal best.

'The exam essay' is a useful 'night before' reminder of how to tackle exam questions, though it will help you more if you also look at it much earlier in the year. 'Model answer' gives an example A-grade essay and the Mind Map and plan used to write it.

The questions

Whenever you come across a question in the guide with a star ✪ in front of it, think about it for a moment. You could make a Mini Mind Map or a few notes to focus your mind. There is not usually a 'right' answer to these: it is important for you to develop your own opinions if you want to get an 'A'. The 'Test' sections are designed to take you about 15–20 minutes each – time well spent. Take a short break after each one.

Line references

Check which version of the play you are studying. The references throughout this guide refer to the Penguin New Shakespeare edition (1996). Note that in that edition Goneril is spelt with two 'l's. In this guide the more usual single 'l' spelling is used.

Key to icons

King Lear is a play with many themes. The most important ones are identified in this guide by icons. These will help you get to grips with your study of the play. The themes represented by each one of the icons below are explained in greater depth in the 'Themes' section.

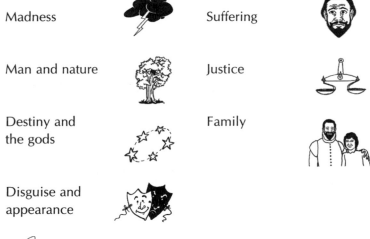

Madness		Suffering	
Man and nature		Justice	
Destiny and the gods		Family	
Disguise and appearance			

LANGUAGE, STYLE AND STRUCTURE

This heading and icon are used in the Commentary wherever there is a special section on the author's choice of words and imagery, and the overall plot structure.

Sources

Most of Shakespeare's plays were based on other sources, or on stories that had already been written down, sometimes as plays. But in every case Shakespeare's genius turned these basic plot sources into something new and far greater than the originals.

The historian Holinshed (died approximately 1580) wrote *The Chronicles of England, Scotland and Ireland*. Shakespeare and other Elizabethan dramatists used stories from this collection as the raw material for plays. The story of Lear was included in the *Chronicles*. Shakespeare's *Macbeth*, another great tragedy, is also based on a Holinshed story.

Lear is a mythical figure. There is no actual historical evidence that he ever lived. But the story had existed in several versions before Shakespeare wrote his great play. It appears in Geoffrey of Monmouth's *Historia Regum Britanniae*, written in the 1300s. In Shakespeare's time the poet Edmund Spenser wrote briefly about Lear and his daughters in his long poem *The Faerie Queen* (1579). There was also a play written in 1594 (approximately ten years before Shakespeare's *King Lear*) by an unknown author, called *The Moste Famouse Chronicle Historye of Leire Kinge of England and His Three Daughters*. Unlike Shakespeare's dark masterpiece, this was a simple melodrama with basic comedy and a happy ending. Cordelia's forces triumph in the battle and Lear is restored to the throne.

None of these earlier versions of the basic story have the Gloucester subplot. Shakespeare may well have derived his inspiration for this from the poet Sir Philip Sidney's long poem *Arcadia*. In this, Sidney recounts the story of a blind king from antiquity who has two sons, one of whom plots against him. When the king realizes this, he wants to throw himself from a cliff.

Finally it is almost certain that Shakespeare knew of an actual event that happened in London when he was a young man working at the theatre there. Sir William Allen, a former mayor of the city, divided his property between his three daughters. His plan was a disaster: all three children treated him dreadfully.

The text

It is not possible to say exactly when Shakespeare sat down and wrote *King Lear*, but experts have fixed its composition as probably late 1605 through to early 1606. The first documented performance was at the court of King James I on Boxing Day 1606.

Theatre, then and now, is a live medium. Scripts are cut and changed as plays are rehearsed and performances evolve. Many plays are never published. The only texts that exist are the scripts used by the actors to learn their lines. This makes the task of finding and printing a word-for-word 'accurate' version (exactly what Shakespeare actually wrote at his desk) of a 400-year-old play like *King Lear* very difficult.

Approximately half of Shakespeare's plays, including *King Lear*, were published during his lifetime in a collection now known as the First Quarto (1608). ('Quarto' refers to the size of the pages of the book, basically small and square.) It is not clear how this collection was composed, but it is certain that the author had nothing to do with preparing the plays for printing. They are known as unauthorized versions. Most of the plays in the First Quarto are not based on Shakespeare's actual manuscripts, but on copies and drafts that were used at the Globe Theatre when the actors were working on the plays. It is thought that the First Quarto version of *King Lear* is based on rough drafts of the play that the boy actors who played Goneril and Regan had kept, plus their memories of what they said on stage!

In 1623, seven years after his death, all Shakespeare's plays were gathered together and published in the First Folio. ('Folio' again refers to the size of the book, which in this case is large and tall.) This was a much better researched 'official' collection of the plays. Of the 1,200 copies printed about 250 still survive. But even in this version of the printed play there may well be changes from what Shakespeare actually wrote, for it is suggested that this text of *King Lear* was based on a revised prompt copy of the play (a copy used by someone who sat beside the stage to 'prompt' actors if they forgot their lines).

There is a particular problem with *King Lear*. There are significant differences between the text of the Quarto and Folio versions of the play. There are roughly 100 lines in the Folio that do not appear in the earlier Quarto, but the Quarto has 300 other lines that are not found in the Folio. Basically the Folio misses out Lear's mock trial of Goneril in the hovel (Act 3, scene 6), the conversation between Cornwall's servants after Gloucester's blinding and the whole of Act 4, scene 3. Lear's last speech also differs in the two versions.

It is impossible to say now which version is the 'true' one, if there ever was one exact text that Shakespeare decided was the definitive version. No copies of the play survive in Shakespeare's own handwriting. Most editions of the play today are based on the Folio, with the missing lines from the Quarto added in. This gives the fullest possible version of the text.

Reading the play

An A-level examiner complained recently that too many students forgot that *King Lear* is a work for performance. Of course you have to study it carefully on the page. You are going to sit an examination and the play is complex and crammed with meaning. The language may not be familiar to you and so close reading is required. But the examiner urged students to remember that the play was designed to be seen on stage. It is important to keep this in mind, to visualize the actors moving about: Edmund strutting, Gloucester shuffling with his face streaming blood. The text is designed to be spoken aloud. You should do this as much as possible to hear the rhythm of the poetry. This will help you to grasp the meaning.

Derek Walcott, the Nobel prize-winning poet and dramatist, once said to the author of this guide:

> You know the great thing about Shakespeare? He wrote for an audience that were standing up in a pit, eating oranges and farting. And he gave them the greatest poetry in the English language, and they loved it.

Shakespeare's theatre was lively, sometimes raucous. Actors shouted to be heard. In *King Lear* they fight, howl and rage. Try to see this in your mind's eye when you read the play. Study it, but use your imagination to bring it to life.

King Lear is an old man who wants to resign the responsibilities of ruling England. He decides to divide his kingdom between his three daughters, Goneril, Regan and Cordelia. The play opens with him inviting each daughter to say how much she loves him. According to their answers they will get a larger or smaller portion of the realm. He expects his favourite and youngest daughter Cordelia to express most love and gain the biggest share. But Cordelia refuses to join in the test, unlike her two sisters. Furious, Lear disowns her and divides his kingdom equally between Goneril and Regan. Of her suitors, only the King of France will accept the disinherited Cordelia without a dowry. She departs with him to France. Kent, a loyal courtier, warns Lear that he is acting foolishly, and he too is banished.

Lear plans to divide his time between the houses of Goneril and Regan, travelling with a train of 100 knights. But the sisters plot to rid themselves of their tiresome and unpredictable father. They deliberately anger him by trying to reduce the number of knights he keeps and finally drive him from Gloucester's castle. Wandering on the wild heath during a terrible storm, Lear has only his Fool, loyal Kent (in disguise) and Gloucester's son Edgar, disguised as a mad beggar, for companions. The storm and Lear both rage and seethe. Lear is driven mad.

The Earl of Gloucester is another elderly man who trusts the wrong child with terrible results. He has a legitimate son, Edgar, and an illegitimate one, Edmund. He loves both equally. But Edmund feels he deserves more, and hatches a plot which successfully persuades Gloucester that Edgar is plotting to kill his father and inherit the earldom. Edgar is forced to flee Gloucester's rage and travel disguised as the madman 'Poor Tom'.

Goneril and Regan discover that Gloucester is sympathetic to Lear's plight, and has gone out into the storm to help his king. They blind Gloucester. He is turned out of his castle but is guided by Edgar towards Dover, where the French army and Cordelia have landed. Gloucester does not recognize his guide as his son. Cordelia intends to restore Lear to the throne.

She and Lear are united at the French camp. Edmund leads the English army against the French and defeats them. He has Lear and Cordelia imprisoned, and sends a death warrant after them.

Goneril and Regan have been competing for Edmund's love. Their rivalry causes Goneril to poison her sister, then kill herself. Edgar appears in disguise after the battle to challenge his brother. Their father Gloucester has died. Edgar mortally wounds Edmund in the fight. Despite the attempts of Goneril's husband Albany to save Lear and his daughter, Cordelia is hanged in prison. Lear dies of grief, cradling Cordelia's corpse, perhaps only half-mad now, knowing more than he can bear of his own foolishness and the cruelty of the world.

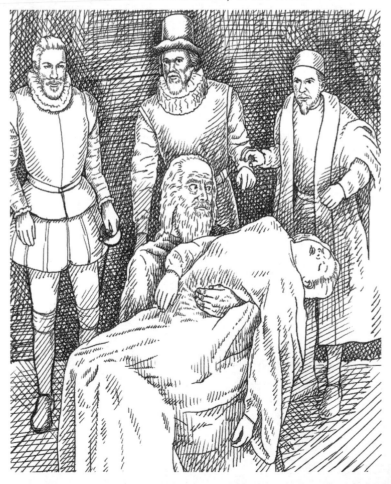

CHARACTERIZATION

The Mini Mind Map above summarizes the main characters in *King Lear*. When you have read this section, look at the full Mind Map on p. 29, then make a copy of the Mini Mind Map and try to add to it from memory.

Lear: *more sinned against than sinning*

King Lear is a complex play full of action, characters in conflict and constantly developing relationships. But the thread that ties everything together is the 'journey' that Lear himself makes: from ruler of a kingdom through madness to a better, more honest and humbler understanding of himself and the world, then finally to his death. Without Lear's decision to hand on and divide his kingdom, none of the other events in the play would occur in the way they do. What happens to Lear is the core around which everything is constructed.

Almost as important as Lear's journey is the parallel thread or subplot of Gloucester and his two sons. We can plot the phases of Lear's and Gloucester's journeys quite clearly through the five Acts of the play. If you understand what happens to these two men and how they are changed, you will have mastered the key themes of what many people regard as Shakespeare's most complex and darkest tragedy.

In Act 1, scene 1, Lear is a powerful ruler presiding over his court. Though old, he is still a man who expects to command everyone else and demands respect. He has a temper that others fear. Note that we learn very little about the sort of king he has been: whether he has ruled wisely and with justice, or if he has made other bad decisions. The one he is about to make will prove catastrophic.

Lear displays terrible rage, disowning his favourite daughter Cordelia because she will not flatter him in the 'love test'. He seems too easily pleased by Goneril and Regan's excessive descriptions of the love they claim to bear him. When Kent urges him to think more carefully about what he is doing, Lear banishes him as well.

❍ Do you think Lear's natural character is fatally flawed, that he is a man who is predisposed to lose his temper when he cannot get his own way? Or do you think years of having the absolute power of a ruler have made him like this? Look at how he behaves throughout the play and make a few notes to support your ideas.

From this starting point in the first scene, we can follow Lear's dramatic journey through the plot.

ACT 1, SCENE 3

We hear that Lear has flown into another rage and hit Goneril's *gentleman* (line 1).

ACT 1, SCENE 4

Lear expresses self-pity. He is concerned only with his own feelings. Though he is affectionate towards the Fool, he is dismissive when he learns the Fool is pining for the banished Cordelia.

This is a key scene for Lear. To begin with Lear will not listen to any criticism. He is sure of his own rightness and authority. But notice that when he clashes with Goneril he questions his own identity, saying:

> *Does Lear walk thus, speak thus. Where are his eyes?*
> *Either his notion weakens, or his discernings*
> *Are lethargied – Ha, sleeping or waking, sure 'tis not so.*
> *Who is it that can tell me who I am?* (lines 223–6)

Although at this point Lear clearly does know who he is, and this speech is usually acted with heavy sarcasm, none the less the sentiment expressed is a dark foretelling of what will happen to Lear later in the play when he really does lose any sense of his own identity.

Later in this scene Lear first admits that he wronged Cordelia, comparing her 'little' crime of not saying how much she loved her father to the much larger wrong he feels Goneril is doing him.

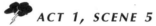 ## ACT 1, SCENE 5

He continues to realize how he treated Cordelia unfairly when, in the middle of a conversation with the Fool, he suddenly says simply *I did her wrong* (line 24). This is also the first scene in which Lear mentions his fear that he may be, or might become, mad.

ACT 2, SCENE 4

Waiting to meet with Regan and Cornwall, Lear is still concerned about maintaining the appearance and rights of a king. The self-obsessed side of his nature is still powerful. But further on in the scene he begins to philosophize on the broader human condition. This is the start of Lear's moving from self-obsession to a wider, bleaker view of mankind generally. This is a crucial shift in his character and it starts when he argues:

> *Oh reason not the need! Our basest beggars*
> *Are in the poorest thing superfluous:*
> *Allow not nature more than nature needs,*
> *Man's life's as cheap as beast's ...* (lines 259–62)

At the same time as he is widening his view of life he is developing a more humble, perhaps more self-pitying view of himself, calling himself *a poor old man* (line 267) instead of a king.

He again mentions his fear of madness in this scene.

ACT 3, SCENE 1

This scene sees the last of Lear's kingly 'power speeches' when he calls down destruction on the world. He attacks hypocrisy and unseen evils. He now appears to have a much bleaker view of man and the world than he did at the start of the play. Hypocrisy and false appearance are powerful themes which obsess him until Act 4, scene 6. He accepts again that he has done Cordelia wrong.

ACT 3, SCENE 4

Lear again talks on broad terms about different degrees of, and responses to, suffering:

> *Thou think'st 'tis much that this contentious storm*
> *Invades us to the skin: so 'tis to thee,*
> *But where the greater malady is fixed*
> *The lesser is scarce felt.* (lines 6–9)

He again repeats his fear that he may go mad. And he again expresses sympathy for the Fool. He is beginning to think more of others than himself. When he does talk of himself, he identifies with the most wretched human beings. Lear raves as a 'genuine' madman, but these outbursts are balanced with many other statements that reveal a new harsh perception of the nature of the world.

ACT 4, SCENE 3

Kent reports that Lear has arrived at Dover where Cordelia is camped with the French army, but he is now so painfully aware of how badly he treated her that he will not see her. Lear has travelled through his madness (and literally journeyed through his kingdom) to arrive at a new, more critical, understanding of his actions and his failings. This new self-awareness is crucial to Lear in the final stage of the play.

ACT 4, SCENE 6

Lear is still mad, but there is a new independence in his attitude. He no longer wants to be flattered and honoured as a king. He rages against evil which he sees everywhere, particularly in women and in the rich and powerful. He understands that appearances can deceive and hide evil. This scene contains the last trace of Lear's madness.

 *ACT 4, SCENE 7*

I am a very foolish fond old man (line 60). This is almost a new Lear, reborn in his reunion with Cordelia. His old, false pride is totally gone. He wishes to make amends to the daughter he has wronged.

ACT 5, SCENE 3

The French army has been defeated but Lear is confident. He has new, more balanced and honest values by which he judges the world. He has a simpler, more joyful view of what matters in life. But the cruellest twist of the plot, Cordelia's death at the moment that Lear has almost come back to his senses as a redeemed man, destroys him. No longer a proud and easily angered tyrant, he dies, grief-stricken but a simpler, wiser and more understanding man. He has made a painful journey that has finally destroyed him. It has been a journey surrounded by violent acts and many deaths, but he has reached a place where he can express true love for his daughter. Lear's view of the world means he understands that it is in the nature of that world to take away the person he most loves so soon after their reconciliation.

In a sense, there could be no way forward for the transformed Lear except death. As the critic A. C. Bradley wrote: 'It seems almost beyond question that any actor is false to the text who does not attempt to express, in Lear's last accents and gestures and look, an unbearable joy.'

✪ For many years it was fashionable to stage an 'alternative' version of the play with a happy ending. The French army defeated Edmund, and Cordelia restored Lear to the throne to rule the country again. Would this be a more satisfying way to end the story? Why? If you think the ending Shakespeare wrote is better, again, why?

Cordelia: *she is herself a dowry*

Cordelia is only 'on stage' at the beginning and the end of the play. Most of the time she is abroad at the court of her new husband, the King of France. Yet her part in the whole tragedy is enormous. Some critics argue that the death of Cordelia is the real tragedy of *King Lear*. Cordelia, they say, is the only truly innocent victim in the whole play. Her execution is the final, awful cruelty that pushes the King towards his death. It means that the play ends with no sense of justice being done.

Cordelia's refusal to take part in the love-test in Act 1, scene 1, is confusing. If she is the most loving, and loved, of the three daughters, why does she not humour her father? Is her refusal to flatter Lear an act of wilful defiance, which, when her sudden acceptance of France as a husband is added to it, sets in motion the whole tragedy of the play? Has she inherited some of her father's stubbornness? Her banishment leaves the stage literally empty for her sisters to occupy. If you take this view of Cordelia's character then it is possible to see her death as a just reward for her early disobedience.

Or is her refusal to flatter a demonstration of her genuine love and honesty? Does she refuse to compete for her father's affections, and a share of his kingdom, because she truly believes her love must be plain and obvious to her father? She is not prepared to compete with her sisters. Note that we are given no clues as to her relationship with Goneril and Regan. Cordelia only ever addresses them directly in one short exchange (Act 1, scene 1, lines 268–82).

In Acts 4 and 5 the 'good' characters make several references to Cordelia's virtuous and honest character. She is well regarded. The 'feminine qualities' of her modest character are much admired. When she is reunited with her father she is respectful and sympathetic, an almost perfect caring and loving daughter. She appears the victim, not the instigator, of the tragedy. This much more sympathetic view of Cordelia makes her death even more painful for both Lear and the audience.

❂ Audience reaction to her death has always been extreme. It is perhaps the most cruel act in the whole play. Do you think it is really necessary, in a story with so many other deaths?

Shakespeare's view of the world and of mankind's inhumanity in *King Lear* is unrelentingly grim throughout, and Cordelia's execution adds enormously to the blackness of the play. It also allows Shakespeare to show, with awful dramatic impact, the ultimate consequence and horror of Lear's foolish actions: the death of the one daughter who truly loved him. It shows Shakespeare's willingness to take risks in creating such a dark plot.

❂ Is Cordelia set up as a paragon of feminine virtues partly to counter-balance the harsh 'manly' characters of Goneril and Regan? Is she truly good, or only in comparison to her sisters?

Goneril and Regan: *tigers, not daughters*

It can be argued that Goneril and Regan are the two characters in the play whom actors have very little freedom to interpret. Shakespeare has written roles which are rigidly, unconditionally evil, cold and vicious. Neither sister ever reveals a softer, even remotely caring side. No tenderness is ever expressed towards their husbands, their father or their sister. At the end of the very first scene they begin to plot their father's downfall. At the end of the play Goneril has poisoned Regan and killed herself, not out of remorse for the murder but because she is thwarted in her passion for Edmund and because her plot to murder her husband is revealed.

A key word often used in describing the sisters is 'unnatural'. This idea would have been particularly striking to Shakespeare's audience. On the Jacobean stage women were almost always portrayed as symbols of feminine virtue: quiet, submissive, morally and practically 'good', and 'pure' in thought and action. Violence and aggression were regarded as male character traits. But Goneril and Regan act violently and aggressively throughout the play. Their own husbands are at times shocked (though Cornwall far less so than Albany) by the depths to which they are prepared to go to destroy Lear and later Gloucester.

Goneril and Regan are often spoken of as a pair, as if they operated in the play like identical twins. But there are considerable and important differences between them. Though they agree to pursue the same general aim – the destruction of

Lear – Goneril is the instigator, Regan initially the follower. Goneril suggests how she and Regan should operate (Act 1, scene 1, lines 285–306) and she sets the plan in motion almost at once by provoking a confrontation with Lear in Act 1, scene 3. Here, she stands up to Lear's rage and gives no ground, providing a terrible contrast to the love she professed to Lear in Act 1, scene 1. Regan, on the other hand, chooses to be away from home when Lear arrives, thereby avoiding a face-to-face conflict.

When Goneril and Albany discuss whether it was wise that she should confront and attack Lear, Goneril completely wins the day. She doesn't even give her husband and his views her full attention: while he is expressing them to her she is calling Oswald to give him fresh instructions to continue the attack on Lear (Act 1, scene 4, lines 310, 324, 330–7). The way Shakespeare has written these lines is an important and dramatic indication of Goneril's character. Her husband is voicing very real concerns over the way she is tempting the fury of a king, while she is busy trying to issue instructions to continue this course of action regardless of his fears, merely answering him between times. She has decided how she is going to act and Albany's concerns barely touch her.

When Regan is confronted by Lear in Act 2, scene 4, she is much more placatory than Goneril. She only begins attacking Lear when her sister arrives. Regan may at this point lack Goneril's 'face-to-face' aggression, but it is Regan who orders the castle door to be locked against Lear not long after. And notice that in Act 2, scene 2, she urges her husband to increase Kent's punishment in the stocks.

By Act 3, scene 7, the sisters are acting with equally matched cruelty in the blinding of Gloucester. Indeed Regan can be said to be in the grip of a blood lust in this most vicious moment in the play. She pulls Gloucester's beard and later stabs and kills the servant who tries to defend him. Swordplay was only ever engaged in by male characters on the Jacobean stage and seeing a woman running a man through, and from behind, must have been truly shocking to Shakespeare's audience.

The actions of Goneril and Regan are so powerfully malicious that they create an avalanche of evil that, to an audience believing in divine retribution, can only call down their eventual destruction. This turns out to be the case when they turn their violence on each other. The sisters both lust after Edmund and the division this creates between them is the cause of their deaths. Their demise is again instigated by Goneril, for it is she who poisons Regan whom she sees as a rival for Edmund's love. Regan is at least a widow by this time, whereas Goneril is happy to engage in an adulterous relationship, and to plot to murder her husband.

Unlike Edmund, the principle anti-hero of the play whose evil is surrounded by an air of heroic defiance, Goneril and Regan are unattractively and coldly evil. Even Edmund comments on them by comparing them to animals, saying they are jealous as *the stung/ Are of the adder* (Act 5, scene 1, lines 56–7).

Shakespeare uses many other animal and monster images when he has characters speak of the sisters, especially Goneril. She is *like a vulture* (Act 2, scene 4, line 130), and a *detested kite* (Act 1, scene 4, line 259). Albany comes to see them as *tigers, not daughters* who behave *like monsters of the deep* (Act 4, scene 2, lines 40 and 49).

Goneril and Regan never repent of their actions, and die in the midst of unnatural enmity towards family members: their father and one another.

✪ Find other examples of animal imagery used to describe Goneril and Regan.

Albany and Cornwall:
a *worthy prince* and a *fiery duke*

There is far more difference between the husbands of Goneril and Regan than there is between the sisters themselves. Broadly speaking, Albany can be described as a weak man who grows to become an honourable one, although arguably out of his depth in the final horrors of the play. He redeems himself by right actions at the end. Cornwall, by contrast, is a villain first and last, capable of great physical cruelty and without any redeeming features. It is a justice of sorts that Albany survives, and grows in stature at the end of the play, while Cornwall lies dead, murdered by a servant.

In the first Act Albany appears as a man who would rather conciliate than confront. He urges the raging Lear to *be patient*

(Act 1, scene 4, line 258) and says, rather weakly given the tension between Lear and Goneril, *My lord, I am guiltless as I am ignorant* (Act 1, scene 4, line 270). He defers to the will of his scheming wife. It is easy to say that Albany is foolish for not seeing the consequences of his wife's harsh determination, but his reluctance to stop her is essential to the plot's development. Albany is absent from the story for the whole of Acts 2 and 3, but when he returns he is a transformed character. Although this long absence makes the change in his character appear to come from nothing, Shakespeare is right not to let us see it happen. Having yet another character undergo a dramatic journey in the play would make the whole thing just too complex and lessen the impact of the changes that happen to Lear and Gloucester.

When Albany reappears in Act 4 he has much more authority. He attacks Regan for what she has done and has become:

> See thyself, devil;
> *Proper deformity shows not in the fiend*
> *So horrid as in woman.* (Act 4, scene 2, lines 59–61)

In the final scene he has the courage to challenge Edmund, then to preside over the duel between him and Edgar. He confronts Goneril with the intercepted letter. Albany's is now the voice of justice and honour. He is stepping in to fill the moral vacuum that Lear created through giving away his kingdom. He is attempting to defeat the evil, and the evil characters, that threaten to overwhelm the troubled kingdom. He has great sympathy for Edgar when he hears of his sufferings as Poor Tom. But he shows no sympathy for those who oppose justice, even when dead:

> *Produce their bodies, be they alive or dead:*
> *This judgement of the heavens, that makes us tremble*
> *Touches us not with pity.* (Act 5, scene 3, lines 228–30)

Albany is a man who has found the voice to speak as a moral and public leader.

> All friends shall taste
> *The wages of their virtue and all foes*
> *The cup of their deservings.* (Act 5, scene 3, lines 300–2)

○ Some critics say that Albany is not really the powerful and authoritative figure he appears to be at the end of the play. He has spent too long deferring to his wife, he has been absent for long periods, and his transformation is 'too little, too late'. What's your view?

If Cornwall has a good side, we never see it. His first practical action is to place the kind and loyal Kent in the stocks, and then defer to Regan's demand to extend the punishment. His tone throughout is arrogant and overbearing. He is instantly drawn to Edmund, the most obviously villainous character in the play. Unlike Albany, he instantly approves of the campaign that Goneril and Regan wage against the Lear and never shows any sympathy for the old man's sufferings. He personally carries out the blinding of Gloucester.

Cornwall's death at the hands of a servant, rather than a more 'worthy' noble opponent, is a brilliant device to heighten the sense of retribution Shakespeare wants us to feel. And there is a neat parallel here: Cornwall turned on Lear when he should have welcomed and protected the old king. Now he is murdered by a servant, a man who should have served and obeyed his master. Cornwall broke the natural social order, just as his servant does in killing him. It is a rare moment of justice in the play. Note also that Shakespeare needed to remove Cornwall from the story quite early on in its development to give space for the rivalry for Edmund's love to develop between the sisters.

○ How does Regan respond to the death of her husband?

Gloucester: a *credulous father*

The fact that Gloucester and Lear are such strikingly distinct characters when so much that happens to them runs parallel is evidence of Shakespeare's brilliance in creating characters. Consider the many points Lear and Gloucester have in common:

- They are both complacent fathers, used to assuming authority within their family.
- They are both fatally deceived by devious and dangerous children.

- They both rashly and ruthlessly attack their good children with very little real evidence, and suffer as a result of their wrong and hasty reactions.
- Both force their loving and loyal children into exile, leaving themselves exposed to attacks from others.
- Both Lear and Gloucester fail to control their households (and probably their kingdom and dukedom) and have to suffer power and authority being taken from them.
- As they endure suffering they both become more generous in their opinions, especially to the absent children they now realize they have wronged.
- Lear is driven mad by the cruelty of his daughters. Gloucester says (Act 3, scene 4, line 159) that thinking about Edgar's (supposed) treachery has driven him *almost mad*.
- Lear has to go through madness before he can understand, Gloucester has to suffer blinding before he can 'see'.
- Their deaths are very similar: both die of broken hearts, but their grief is overlaid with joy. It is unbearable, contrasting emotions that stop their old hearts.

So is Gloucester just a smaller version of Lear? Is Gloucester's journey – believing a false son, causing the loyal one to flee, realizing his mistake, suffering horribly for it, losing his authority and power, gaining new insights though literally blind, travelling (like Lear) to Dover and dying there – just a mirror for Lear's story? Absolutely not. By establishing several significant differences, Shakespeare makes Gloucester a distinct figure in his own right.

At the beginning of the play Gloucester is a much more affable and morally lightweight figure than Lear. He tells Kent he has a bastard son and seems almost proud of his past promiscuity. He does not seem to have displayed much kindness towards Edmund, although he professes to love him as much as his legitimate son.

Gloucester is the most superstitious character in a play where superstition is an important element. Although many people in the Jacobean audience would have been deeply superstitious, Shakespeare may be using Gloucester's appalling *naïveté* and bad judgement to criticize astrology and superstition, and those who believe in them.

A very obvious difference between Lear and Gloucester is that Lear is never afraid to confront anyone face to face, whereas Gloucester is a weaker figure, at least to begin with. When Kent is put in the stocks, Gloucester tries to press the case that he is Lear's messenger, but not very powerfully. Gloucester is loyal to Lear, but he appears to be afraid of angering Cornwall. When Regan orders the doors of Gloucester's own castle to be shut against Lear he barely comments on the cruelty of her actions.

But Gloucester becomes, if not heroic, then at least admirable when he finally risks danger and goes out into the storm to help Lear. And he does become brave and heroic in Act 3, scene 7, when he attacks Goneril and Regan to their faces. Gloucester is not a naturally heroic figure, but he has stood his ground, and suffered terribly for it. It is impossible, having witnessed his blinding, not to feel pity for him as he is led towards Dover.

But whereas Lear does rise to a new understanding after his madness, and definitely dies a better man, Gloucester never really recovers from his torture. He feels he is drowning in a sea of suffering. Lear moves from the personal to the public, Gloucester never does. He attempts to commit suicide. The manner he chooses and the way Edgar, in disguise, prevents him actually harming himself, is one of the most bizarre events in the play and hardly presents Gloucester in a way that makes us think him heroic. It is the action of a defeated and confused man. He does, however, attain some form of redemption before his death. He comes to understand the world in a clearer way, though compared to Lear in a very limited and personally focused way.

✪ How does Gloucester's treatment of Edgar at the start of the play compare to Lear's treatment of Cordelia?

Edgar: *a brother noble*

Many critics complain that Edgar is not a fully rounded character but a series of roles necessary for the plot. After appearing only briefly as himself, he spends most of the play disguised as the mad beggar Poor Tom and later as a country rustic. At the end of the play he has outgrown his role as a loyal though rather too trusting son to become a man of decision and authority. He, Kent and Albany are the only survivors who have never been tainted by the evil through which they have lived. Edgar could well inherit the kingdom.

Edgar may be too much of a chameleon for us to relate to him in the same way as we might do Edmund, but he performs a vital role in the play, acting as link between the main (Lear family) plot line and the subplot of Gloucester and his sons. As Poor Tom he delivers several cleverly worded speeches that act upon both Gloucester and Lear, who see the truth behind his apparent ramblings.

Edgar's complete trust in Edmund (with whom he has not been in close contact for nine years) seems rather foolish and naïve, and this weakness of character is further suggested on two occasions, once when he says his disguise is threatened by uncontrolled tears (Act 3, scene 6, lines 59–60) and once when he says in an aside that he cannot continue to pretend in the face of his father's pain.

Edgar does reveal his character to be stronger and better founded than the beginning of the play may suggest. He hardly complains of the suffering he has to endure, and shows unflagging concern for Lear and Gloucester. He makes the most of difficult circumstances which suggests he is a resilient person. He delights in beating Oswald and does not hesitate to challenge Edmund, whom we can assume to be a formidable opponent. And we must remember that Jacobean audiences would recognize in Edgar's acceptance of Edmund's word a common device used in theatre of the time: good characters were always easily fooled – a trusting nature was part of their goodness. It was evil characters who were suspicious of others.

Another traditional device which the audience would have had in their minds while watching Edgar in the later stages of the play was that revengers are usually sinister characters. Edgar is going to exact revenge on Edmund, but Shakespeare makes sure that Edgar shows noble charity after the fight. As he explains his story to Albany and Edmund, goodness and moral worth are clearly presented to the audience.

The really curious thing in Edgar's part in the story is that he chooses not to reveal himself to his father until a mere half hour before the old man's death. While Edgar initially dons a disguise to avoid his father's fury, once Gloucester is blind and virtually incapable there can be little point in continuing with it. ✪ What reason do you think Edgar might have for this delay?

Edgar has endured awful hardships and been misrepresented by one he trusted to one he loved. He has grown in strength of character as a result of his trials and tribulations.

> **Edmund:** *now gods, stand up for bastards!*

Two of the finest speeches in the whole play are Edmund's and, apart from a couple of polite replies at the start of Act 1, scene 1, they are his opening words. Few characters in any Shakespeare play introduce themselves with such magnificent and forceful poetry.

In the first speech, Act 1, scene 2, lines 1–22, Edmund reveals the drive and energy of his personality in a scathing attack on the moral order that makes him a bastard and his brother legitimate. He is aggrieved that he is treated as the lesser son (although Gloucester has told Kent he treats both his sons as equals). He states his intentions bluntly and coldly, *Well, then,/ Legitimate Edgar, I must have your land* (lines 15–16).

He also states *Thou Nature, art my goddess; to thy law/ My services are bound* (lines 1–2) which presents us with one of the key themes of the play. Edmund will commit a series of dreadful acts, will ignore moral codes and restrictions, and do all this without disguise, remorse or apology. He claims that he is simply acting according to nature. But note that in the quote Nature is personified. It is not his own nature he is referring to, but his own nature as part of Nature, the natural order. Much of the play is about the reality of Nature, and Shakespeare presented a much bleaker view of the natural order than many in his audience would have expected. So in this first speech Edmund is sounding a note that will echo through the whole play.

Later in the scene, after he has set the deception of his father in motion, Edmund gives a second great speech. Unlike the first speech this one is in prose and is a wonderful wide-ranging attack on people who believe in astrology. He mocks

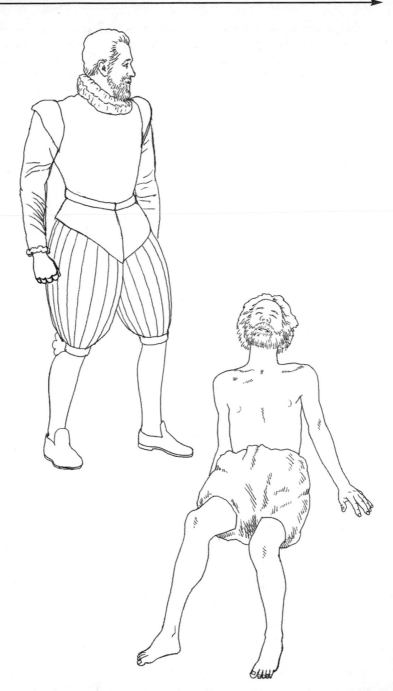

the hypocrisy of people who blame their faults on the influence of adverse astrological conjunctions. The result of these two speeches is to present Edmund as a giant of rage and anger, but with a cold intelligence that makes his speeches go far beyond mere rant. He is self-confident, proud, independent and ready to sweep all conventions and restrictions aside to gain what he wants.

✪ Compare the evil of Edmund to that of Goneril and Regan. How would you describe the difference between them?

Edgar is almost admirable in his evil, and indeed it may be that Shakespeare intended us to 'admire' elements of his personality, so that we would be more shocked when the merciless drive of his character causes him to deliver Gloucester to Cornwall and Regan and later to issue the death warrant upon Lear and Cordelia.

Some critics have noted an element of self-deception in Edmund. Though he professes to loath the society that keeps him on the edge of things and denies him equality with Edgar, he uses all force and means to try to gain exactly those benefits that society bestows: power, title and wealth. But we should note that it is the conventional attitudes and hypocrisy of society that Edmund detests, not its rewards and comforts.

Wounded and dying, Edmund does repent, which is curious given the force with which he expresses his evil intentions at the start of the play. It seems too quick and easy. A man with his energy and confidence might have faced death defiant and unbowed. ✪ Why do you think Edmund repents? What would the effect be if Edmund had died still professing his beliefs in the rule of nature and unreconciled with Edgar?

The Fool: *a bitter fool*

Classical Greek theatre used the device of a chorus, extra voices who were not characters operating within the plot but who observed what was happening and commented upon it or added explanations for the audience. The Fool is a one-man chorus, albeit a rather wild and (to contemporary ears) sometimes confusing one, rather than a fully developed character. We learn that he pines for Cordelia after she is banished, that Lear is very fond of the Fool, and we may feel sympathy for him when he cowers in the storm. But apart from these small points, the Fool exists only as a function of the plot. When his work – to accompany Lear on his journey through madness – is complete, he vanishes without comment or explanation. This may have been a practical necessity for Shakespeare. Women's roles were played by young men or boys and theatre records suggest that the same actor may have been cast to play both the Fool and Cordelia. On the other hand, the Fool is supposed to be quite elderly, having been with Lear for many years, which makes this doubling difficult to imagine. Today of course, Cordelia is always played by a woman, and so this doubling never occurs. So we are left to ponder why the Fool vanishes.

✪ What role in the plot could the Fool serve after the point at which he leaves the story?

Despite an endless repertoire of jokes, riddles, snatches of songs and pieces of advice, careful reading of the Fool's words to Lear reveal him to be offering good advice and sound judgement throughout. He uses humour to tell harsh truths. Along with Kent and Cordelia, the Fool is a voice of reason and good advice. His is a voice as uncompromisingly honest as Kent's. He constantly picks at Lear, reminding him again and again how foolishly he has acted in giving away his kingdom. Lear clearly understands that the Fool can speak wisely, for he threatens him with the whip if he keeps harping on about Lear's foolishness. The Fool's sarcasm cuts Lear to the quick. For his part Lear is clearly fond of the Fool: it is to him that Lear calls out when he fears he is going mad.

Some critics have said that the Fool's constant attacks on Lear for his dreadful judgement help drive Lear insane. This may be deliberate. The Fool is more wise than he appears. He may know he has to drive Lear through a dark night of madness in order for the king to arrive at an understanding that will allow him to be reconciled with the daughter he has wronged. Goneril may set Lear's anguish in motion, but the Fool's constant barbs and jibes certainly drive him into greater torments.

The Fool also speaks his opinions in a more public way towards the end of his time in the story, making him even more of a voice of comment and reason. The prophecy he gives in Act 3, scene 2, lines 79–94 can be read as a comment on the wrongs of Lear's reign (in which case they are the only 'evidence' we have of the quality of Lear's kingship). The Fool may be providing the audience with a vital piece of background information. He is certainly speaking directly to them, not Lear, at this point. It is the last long speech the Fool makes, and can be seen as a significant 'signing off' of the chorus. His commentary is replaced by the calmer but still scattered utterances of Poor Tom. They don't share the stage for long: a madman and a Fool together is too much.

We must remember that the Fool's songs and jokes would have appealed as light relief to the groundlings in the pit of Shakespeare's theatre. Many of the jokes that are obscure to us would have been genuinely funny to them and the Fool would have provided laughter in an otherwise dark and cruel story. His cavortings help defuse dramatic situations that could otherwise become too relentlessly bleak. There is only so much despair that an audience can take, and at times when that point is approached the Fool inevitably interjects some wild or comic moment. ❂ Find examples of the Fool doing this in Act 3.

Some commentators regard the Fool as the good son Lear never had. ❂ What do you think of this view?

Kent: *'tis my occupation to be plain*

Unlike Lear, Gloucester, Albany or Edgar, Kent makes no 'journey' during the play. He does not develop or change: he remains throughout plain-speaking, honest and loyal to his king. With so many manipulative and evil people abroad in the kingdom, he stands as a symbol of the old order. Notice how, during Act 1, scene 1, even though he speaks bluntly to Lear, he starts by addressing him respectfully as *my liege* or *my lord*. When he begins to defend Cordelia from her father's rash judgements he still uses many deferential terms, calling the king *Royal Lear, father, master, great patron* (lines 139–42). But when Lear refuses to change his mind Kent calls him bluntly *old man*. This shows both Kent's courage (for he knows Lear's capacity for rage) and the concern he feels for what has happened. We assume that up to this point Kent has been a loyal attendant on Lear during his reign.

Kent can be described as representing the ideal of the yeoman of England: plain men who serve the king. He is unfailingly sound in his judgements, accepts punishment (from Cornwall and Regan) without complaint, and thinks only of Lear's distress when they are out in the storm. He is brave, not hesitating to beat Oswald (on two separate occasions). He speaks his mind in any company. When challenged by Cornwall, Regan, Gloucester and their followers to explain why he has attacked Oswald (in Act 2, scene 2) Kent says simply:

> *Sir, 'tis my occupation to be plain:*
> *I have seen better faces in my time*
> *than stands on any shoulder that I see*
> *before me at this instant.* (lines 90–4)

The risk of offending a duke, an earl and the king's daughter will not stop Kent from speaking his mind. When we hear this speech we begin to guess that Kent will be proved right: these people will not behave honourably. Kent is always correct in his judgement.

But there is a definite falling off of Kent's energy in the final two Acts. It is as if he is a barometer for Lear's decline and the world Lear represents. Kent knows that the battle between Edmund's forces and the French army will determine his future, and we sense that he knows the day may well go against him when he says:

> *My point and period will be thoroughly wrought*
> *Or well or ill, as this day's battle fought.*
>   (Act 4, scene 7, lines 95–6)

Kent performs a vital role in the plot by keeping us informed of events 'off stage', and by explaining (probably for those members of the audience who needed a bit of extra explanation!) the importance of events that were developing in the plot. He does this by conversations with 'a Gentleman' in

Act 3, scene 1, and Act 4, scene 3. (In some editions it is a 'Knight' whom Kent meets in Act 3.)

Kent contrives a disguise in order to serve Lear even though he has been banished. As his whole purpose is to serve the king, Kent is a disappointed man (*I hope to die*) in the final scene when, at the moment when he can reveal himself, the king dies. But until this point he has injected positive energy and common sense into a play that is otherwise almost entirely dark and cruel in its mood.

Oswald: *a knave, a rascal*

Oswald exists principally as a servant of Goneril, not as a fully developed person in his own right. A minor character, he is none the less important to the plot. He carries out Goneril's commands, including being insolent to Lear at the start of the sisters' campaign against their father. There are several instances in Jacobean theatre of servants reflecting the characters of their masters or mistresses, and Oswald is, in his own smaller way, driven, like Goneril, by malice and evil. He seeks reward from her as keenly as she covets the kingdom.

Oswald is insolent, dishonest, and a coward. His cowardice is wonderfully drawn out in Act 2, scene 2, where Kent abuses him with probably the most spectacular outburst of insults in any Shakespeare play (lines 12–22), then draws his sword to fight. Oswald by comparison says hardly a word in his own defence, then runs and cries *Help, ho! Murder, help* (line 37).

❂ Why is the contrast between the personalities of Kent and Oswald important to the plot?

Know your characters

? Make a list of all the characters we have looked at in the 'Characterization' section. Write beside each name what you think is the main motive that drives them in the play.

Your motive right now is a need to relax — take a break.

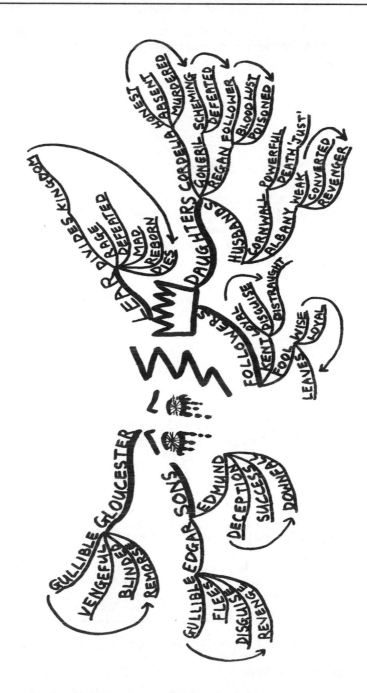

29

THEMES

Themes are ideas explored by the play, but not actually part of the mechanics of the plot. They are the universal ideas that underlie what happens; the broader messages of the play. For example, Lear's madness is a crucial element in the tragic story of the king and his daughters. His descent into insanity is a vital part of the way the plot unfolds. But Shakespeare intended many of the comments on madness, and those Lear makes in his ravings about the world, to be seen as truths going far beyond the world of his play. Lear raves about particular injustices that he suffers, but the audience can read into his words much wider comments on injustice, and madness, in the world in general.

King Lear is a play with many themes. The most important ones are identified in the 'Characterization' and 'Commentary' sections of this book with icons (see 'Key to icons', p. xiv). The Mind Map below shows the seven main themes.

Madness

Jacobean audiences were used to seeing mad characters on stage as comic figures. Their antics were used to bring light relief to scenes. In *King Lear* Shakespeare does something daring and innovative. His main character goes insane, and though he raves and has delusions, there is a savage wisdom in his 'mad' views of the world and mankind. In the character of Lear, Shakespeare is giving us a serious and painful portrayal of madness. Remember it was common for members of his audience to have a day out at London's Bedlam (Bethlehem) lunatic asylum to laugh at the antics of the inmates. In *King Lear* they saw a great man reduced to a lunatic, then recovering to become a changed and better person. They were presented with a more complex account of madness than they had ever seen before.

Lear's journey through insanity is the core of the play. Through madness Lear learns a new way of looking at himself and the world. He re-evaluates the human condition, and finds the world a much harsher place than it seemed when he was a king. But he does come to see what is really of value and dies in some ways a better man for the revelation. Lear's madness is a personal event that happens to a father driven mad by suffering, an old man who was once a king reduced to a homeless, witless wanderer. But we must see in his journey a much wider theme being presented to us, about truth and falsehood, superficiality and value. For Lear to undergo such a radical transformation in the play, a descent into insanity and a recovery (of sorts) is the only means by which this could happen. Lear is stripped of everything, materially, intellectually and spiritually, and 'rebuilt' by the forgiveness and love of Cordelia into someone almost entirely different, and certainly better.

Madness was a standard device in theatre of Shakespeare's time. Characters descended into chaos before order was restored, their madness abated and they re-emerged into the drama changed, usually for the better.

For a more detailed account of the stages of Lear's journey through madness, see the notes on him in the 'Characterization' section.

Apart from Lear, there are other types and degrees of madness in the play, all of them vital to the story and the themes.

The verbal and physical violence of Goneril, Regan and Cornwall is a form of psychopathic blood lust. As the play progresses they appear to lose control of their own thirst for violence and thereby hasten their own downfall. The blinding of Gloucester (Act 3, scene 7) is the point at which they descend into uncontrolled savagery. Cornwall receives his fatal wound from a servant appalled at the hideous cruelty.

✪ Edmund, at least as violent as the sisters and Cornwall, does not share their blood lust. How mentally stable do you think he is?

Another kind of madness in the play is the Fool's professional role-playing. But the Fool's wandering speeches, jokes, riddles and snatches of songs have a very clear 'method in their madness'. He makes many appropriate and cutting points in his quips and comments about Lear's predicament and the world in general.

Edgar's faked madness in the role of Poor Tom again brings up the issue of insanity. But we know that Edgar is acting, and Shakespeare could well have wanted Poor Tom to be initially laughed at by the audience to bring a little light relief to this otherwise dark phase of the story. But Shakespeare makes the audience confront the harsh reality of what they might laugh at in real life. They may find Tom somewhat comical to begin with, but then gradually there comes a creeping sense of guilt. When Tom talks of the hardships of his life, and when he talks of being driven close to suicide by invisible demons, it is impossible for the audience not to pity someone so impoverished and deluded.

Finally Gloucester's anguish is so great that it can be said to be a form of madness which drives him to seek suicide.

Suffering

The relentless suffering in *King Lear* is awful, harrowing, violent and almost, for characters, and audiences sometimes, unendurable. It drives Lear to madness and he continues to suffer while mad. Gloucester suffers physically and mentally and is driven almost mad with grief and remorse.

But it is important to see suffering as separate from, though a part of, madness. And it is not just the mad who suffer. Edgar suffers dreadfully watching his father in his blind agony. The Fool suffers physically during the storm. We can imagine that the exiled and disinherited Cordelia suffers while 'off stage' away in France. Kent suffers, quietly and stoically as is his character, but tragically, to the point where, at the end of the play, he longs for his own death.

The play is full of images describing mental torment and suffering in terms of physical pain. Lear's tears *scald* him, his shame *burns*. Goneril and Regan's treatment of him has left him *cut to the brains* (Act 4, scene 6, line 194). As his madness leads him to have a wider and more compassionate view of the world he speaks eloquently and sympathetically of the suffering of the poor and wronged of the world.

This detailing of suffering beyond the immediate plot of the play is picked up by Edgar, who gives a grim account of the suffering of the madman he pretends to be. Again this must be Shakespeare making his audience aware of the reality of the madness they were used to laughing at (see previous section on 'Madness'). Though Edgar has to establish a credible character as Tom, he gives powerful, moving speeches through Act 3, scene 4, describing the pains and privations of Tom, the wandering and despised madman, that could be said to have far more heart and feeling in them than the plot device of Edgar's disguise really requires. The pitiful line *Who gives anything to Poor Tom* (line 49) is heart-breaking in its cruel simplicity. He goes on to describe his suffering in a vivid list. Further on in the same scene he gives another tragic account of the madman's lot *whipped from tithing to tithing and stocked, punished and imprisoned* (lines 128–9).

Suffering is always at the forefront of Shakespeare's view of man's experience in this play. The question 'Where does this suffering come from, men's actions or the gods?' is a bigger question dealt with more fully in the 'Destiny and the gods' section below.

Man and nature

Nature is a complex idea in *King Lear*. It has several linked meanings:

- Nature as in the natural world, as opposed to the world of man. The play is dominated by one huge natural image: the storm. Nature here is shown as a violent force able to destroy even a king. It is pitiless.

- Nature as in the natural order among man: the rules of family and society. Nature in this sense is pulled apart by the conspiracy of children against parents.
- Nature as in the natural disposition or character of individuals. Characters acting contrary to their true natures (Goneril, Regan, Edmund), or the natures they should have, are a key source of drama throughout the play.

The link between a man's nature and the natural order is most clearly expressed by Edmund in his key speech in Act 1, scene 2. He begins with the battle cry *Thou nature art my goddess; to thy law/ My services are bound* (lines 1–2). 'Nature' has a complex meaning here. He is appealing to the natural order, perhaps the 'law of the jungle' to be his guide. He is also saying that he will be honest to his own nature, meaning his character.

There is an abundance of animal images throughout the play. Most of these images portray nature as vicious and uncaring. Goneril is described as *a vulture* (Act 2, scene 4, line 130), and the sisters together as *pelican daughters* (Act 3, scene 4, line 72): it was commonly believed in Shakespeare's time that young pelicans attack and kill their father. The Fool compares Lear's plight to *The hedge sparrow that fed the cuckoo so long/ That it's had its head bit off by the young* (Act 1, scene 4, lines 211–12). And Lear, lamenting over Cordelia's body asks *Why should a dog, a horse, a rat have life/ And thou no breath at all?* (Act 5, scene 3, lines 304–5): nature is cruel in letting mere animals live while his daughter lies murdered.

All this suggests that nature, both in the sense of the creatures of the world and the natural way of the world, is a cruel entity. But there is another line of appeal to nature made in the play which suggests that it can be a benign force and that much of the evil that happens does so because characters act out of nature. There is a natural order which they break. Children turn on parents, violence of 'unnatural' savagery is let loose.

There are many references which imply that nature is a supportive force for good. Gloucester, when Edgar's 'conspiracy' is first revealed by Edmund, calls the latter *a loyal and natural boy* (Act 2, scene 1, line 83). Conversely, Lear appeals to the benign view of nature when he turns on Cordelia in Act 1, scene 1, and calls her a *wretch whom Nature is ashamed/ Almost to acknowledge hers* (lines 212–13).

It is difficult to decide whether Shakespeare wanted us to see nature as 'good' or 'evil'. Nature is powerful, often destructively so, and can be a source of good or evil. If there is a final word on nature in *King Lear*, it is probably that nature is a force for harm when the natural order is broken. And man is part of nature, so man's 'nature' (in the sense of character and disposition) is part of the natural world.

○ Draw a Mini Mind Map showing the various elements of the concept of nature in *King Lear* (put the word nature in the centre of the Map).

Justice

In many of Shakespeare's other tragic plays justice is clearly and unequivocally seen to be done by the end of the story. Hamlet kills Claudius, who murdered Hamlet's father and took his wife and his throne. Macbeth is finally killed by the man whose family have perhaps suffered most in Macbeth's ruthless rise to power. But although the forces of good triumph in *King Lear*, the most innocent and 'virtuous' person in the story, Cordelia, is murdered and her father suffers terribly, then dies of grief. There is no happy ending for anyone. This lack of justice, in the conventional sense at least, contributes hugely to this play being the bleakest and most harrowing of any Shakespeare work. Though the villains do die, they leave behind a world shattered by the legacy of their evil.

There are many other references to justice clearly designed to be read as comments on the wider concept of fairness in the world beyond the play. Lear's mock trial of his daughters at the height of his madness in Act 3, scene 4, both moves the plot forward by showing us simultaneously the depth and cause of his insanity, and can also be seen as Shakespeare commenting upon the absurdities, the madness, of some legal processes in the wider world.

Similar comments are made, again by Lear, in Act 4, scene 6, in his speech against the hypocrisy of the world (lines 160–9).

Here he picks out for special condemnation the (court) beadle and the *robes and furred gowns* (of judges) that hide infamy.

In addition to justice in the sense of fairness and the law, ideas about judgement occur throughout the play. Usually the results of judgements are disastrous. Lear's judgements of his daughters are completely wrong, Gloucester's judgement of his sons is equally hopeless. Kent, one of the fairest and most just characters in the play, is subject to a punishment Jacobean audiences would instantly recognize from their own lives, the stocks.

However, some critics argue that there is a type of harsher, cruel justice that does operate 'fairly' in the play. Lear is punished with madness for his sins against Cordelia, Gloucester with blindness for his actions against Edgar. The principal villains, Cornwall, Edmund, Goneril and Regan, all die. This form of resolution has nothing to do with the kind of justice dispensed by a court of law. It is a more cruel and final settlement of scores.

Destiny and the gods

This theme explores a key idea in Jacobean thought and theatre. Were human beings in 'real life', and the characters in a play, completely in charge of their actions and their destiny? Or were they ultimately able only to act according to their preordained natures? Did they have free will or were their lives, or at least their natures, already laid out and unchangeable?

In *King Lear*, Edmund could be said to make the case for free will. He tells us in Act 1, scene 2, that he will take charge of his life to get what he wants, and no one will stand in his way. Gloucester appears to hold the opposite view. In the same scene he suggests that lives are controlled by bigger forces, which is why he is so depressed by the bad omens that people claim to have seen.

The free will versus destiny debate is a complex philosophical issue. For the purposes of your Shakespeare study, you do not need to spend too much time trying to make up your mind about it. However, the tension between the two opposing views is a powerful theme throughout the play and you need to recognize its importance. It is another layer of conflict in the plot.

Note the plural in the heading: *gods*. The world of *King Lear* is pagan. Remember that the Fool locates the play as being before Merlin's time (Act 3, scene 3, line 95), before Christianity existed. There is no Christian God in the play, but certain characters, especially Gloucester, speak of supernatural deities believed to control events on earth. He maintains that the suffering he endures is caused by sadistic gods. Edmund demands that the gods *stand up for bastards!* (Act 1, scene 2, line 22). There are other references to the gods having influence over events. But notice that none of the characters who complain about the malign interventions of gods appear to worship them in any conventional Christian sense. The gods are simply facts of existence. Lear asks the gods to punish Goneril and Regan when they turn against him. He sees them as a force to be used to intervene for his benefit, but he does not pray to them.

If most characters believe the gods can wield this sort of power, then Edmund's speech at the beginning of Act 1, scene 2, is even more powerful because (despite the appeal quoted above) he is defying conventional belief. But notice that Edmund does profess to worship nature, whether the concept of nature or his own nature is debatable. Dying, he shows no interest in any god that he may be about to meet. His change of heart is apparently a purely human decision, not prompted by a sudden religious conversion.

If the gods control the actions of man, then are men less responsible, less free, than they think? This question runs right through the play as a background idea. It links to the notion of justice, for if the gods have power over men on earth then their influence must contribute to the justice or injustice in the play.

Cordelia, Edgar and Albany are the only characters in this pagan story who appear to have beliefs in gods with virtues that a Jacobean audience would instantly recognize as a least similar to those of the Christian faith. Edgar says *The gods are just* (Act 5, scene 3, line 168). Cordelia calls on *you kind gods* (Act 4, scene 7, line 14) to restore her father's sanity. Albany hopes that while Cordelia is in prison *The gods defend her* (Act 5, scene 3, line 254). These characters seem to revere the gods much more readily than the others, and to seek their benign intervention. They appear to believe in gods who are basically protective and caring. But then the very next action after Albany's utterance is the arrival of a grief-stricken Lear carrying Cordelia's body. These most nearly-Christian benign gods do not seem to have heard Albany.

❂ Some critics have argued that Cordelia's murder, cruelly wiping out the case that the gods are good, suggests that *King Lear* is a play which promotes an atheistic viewpoint. Do you think this is true?

Critics have long studied the balance between free will and fate in *King Lear*. There is no easy answer. It seems that in the world of the play there is a shifting balance between men being able to shape their own futures (as Edmund, Goneril and Regan do in the first half of the play) and being mere pawns of pagan gods.

❂ What lines can you find that suggest that life is preordained? What examples are there supporting the concept of free will?

Family

Relationships between parents and children and between siblings are at the core of the plot of *King Lear*. The main plot and the subplot of the play both focus on what happens when children turn against parents. Although in *King Lear* this results in a kingdom torn apart and in numerous deaths, the basic conflict of the story is a version of a simple and ordinary situation: what aged parents expect from their children and the reactions of their children to these expectations. This is a timeless dramatic opportunity, the point where power is shifting from one generation to the next.

Lear demands gratitude. When Cordelia refuses to honour him with extravagant overtures of love, he rages. When Goneril and Regan begin to wear him down with their refusal to honour him, he rages. This rage at the injustice he sees in his children's ingratitude is what drives him to madness.

Cordelia and Edgar are part of the 'old' order as represented by their respective ageing fathers and Kent. They love their parents, bear no grudge for the wrongs done them, and honour the elderly, faults and all. Goneril, Regan and Edmund on the other hand are the young order, full of (usually vicious) energy and unwilling to wait for power and position to pass naturally to them. In a sense they are the modernists, the self-serving revolutionaries who want their future, now!

We are given tantalizingly few hints as to what sort of ruler Lear was, or whether Gloucester was a parent who deserved honour and respect. But the little evidence there is, combined with the rage and 'unnatural' fury and punishment both men unleash on their children (Lear on Cordelia, Gloucester on Edgar), suggest that neither old man was a model parent. For the system of respect towards elders to operate successfully, the elders have to be worthy of respect. They have duties towards their children.

We cannot but ask, however quietly, whether Goneril, Regan and, especially, Edmund, are not at least a little justified in their demands at the start of the play. Their future deeds may render the question irrelevant, but it is still an issue to consider at the beginning of the story. The question is complex and debatable, and this again accounts in part for the timeless relevance of the story of *King Lear* and his three daughters, of Gloucester and his two sons.

Note that no one ever refers to the wives of Lear or Gloucester. We know nothing about the mothers of their children, except that illegitimate Edmund's was *fair* (Act 1, scene 1, line 21).

Disguise and appearance

Disguise is a major element in the complex plot of *King Lear*:

- Edgar spends most of the play in various disguises;
- Kent also spends the whole of Acts 2, 3 and 4 in disguise;
- The Fool is always in his professional role, another form of disguise, which allows him special licence to challenge Lear.

Disguise allows Kent to continue to follow Lear although he has been banished. It allows Edgar to escape the fury of his father, and then to guide him to safety. Without people being disguised the mechanics of the plot would break down.

There is another, less literal and deeper level of disguise in the play. People appearing to be different from their true natures is also vital to the plot. Goneril and Regan appear (in Act 1, scene 1) to be good and loving daughters. Likewise Edmund (Act 1, scene 2) appears to be the good and caring son. These characters are disguising their true natures. The image people present of themselves and the difference between this and their true natures is a key theme. In the cases of Goneril, Regan and Edmund, that which is hidden is much darker and more dangerous than their public face.

Occurrences of misreading appearances are equally important in the play. Lear fails to see Goneril and Regan for what they really are until it is too late, Gloucester likewise with Edgar and Edmund.

Try this

? The Fool is a wise man who disguises his wisdom in his role as a jester. Do you think this is an example of another form of disguise? Make a Mind Map to explore this idea.

The Fool said that when his work was over he would go to bed at noon. Don't go that far, but take a break now.

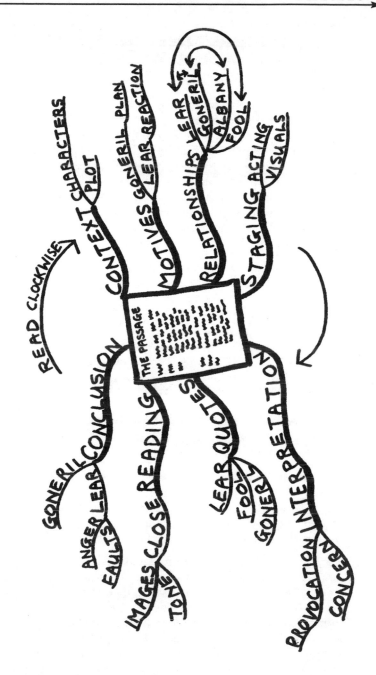

Poetry and prose

Three-quarters of *King Lear* is written in blank verse; that is, in **iambic pentameter** – lines of ten syllables divided into five pairs of unstressed/stressed syllables. This creates a regular pattern of sound, of alternating unstressed (soft) and stressed (hard) syllables when read aloud. The lines rarely rhyme, though there are pairs of rhyming couplets at the end of some scenes which are used to give a sense of closing. Look at the last lines of the play:

> *The oldest hath borne most; we that are young*
> *Shall never see so much, nor live so long.*

Count the syllables. Read the lines aloud and hear where the regular beats fall to create a steady rhythm.

Many of the great speeches in the play are written in this form of verse. The rhythm gives a sense of grandeur and structure to the actor's lines. And don't forget that ultimately Shakespeare wrote all this great poetry for actors to deliver live on stage. This is a play to be heard by an audience, not a long poem to be studied on the page. But because the language is so dense, so packed with meaning, both about the plot and about the themes of the play, it is vital that we study certain aspects of it.

Shakespeare switches from poetry to prose throughout the play to achieve certain definite dramatic effects. His audience would instantly note that the words they were hearing were no longer in rhythmic verse and the actors would no doubt have emphasized the shift by changing their way of delivering the lines.

Very few plays are written in verse today but for Shakespeare's audience this was the most common type of language heard on stage. They would have understood that, traditionally, prose was used in plays for exchanges between servants (often with humorous exaggerated accents), comic scenes, for reading letters, making proclamations and sometimes for 'asides' to the audiences when characters revealed their thoughts and feelings. Broadly speaking, prose sounded less refined than poetry and so was usually given to 'lower' characters: servants, clowns and madmen.

But Shakespeare breaks these traditional rules to great effect throughout *King Lear*. Lear himself has a great number of lines in prose, especially in his mad scenes. His shift to prose signifies his descent from greatness. Other characters who are debased by the story, such as Edgar and Kent who have to assume disguises, also 'fall' from poetry to prose for the same reason.

Using both rhythmic poetry and less structured, more flowing prose also creates interesting dramatic contrasts in the sound of the play. In the first scene Kent and Gloucester 'chat' as two experienced men of the world (Act 1, scene 1, lines 1–23): though their conversation is important to the plot, it contains neither great proclamations nor intense emotion. It flows along easily in prose. But when Lear enters in all his majesty and declares his intentions (lines 36–54) he speaks in poetry, for this is a king making a vital pronouncement.

❍ At the end of this scene Goneril and Regan talk quietly together in prose. What is the dramatic effect of returning to prose here after so much poetry during the high drama of this long scene?

Contrasts between poetry and prose occur throughout the play. They occur in Act 3, scene 2 – the storm scene – where Lear's whirling and ranting poetry is set against the comic prose of the Fool. Edgar speaks mostly in prose when he pretends to be Poor Tom because this is a lowly figure whose role does not allow him the 'greatness' or nobility of poetry, but Edgar's asides and soliloquies, not heard by other characters, are in verse. This reminds us that he is a nobleman in disguise. So even his style of language as Poor Tom is part of Edgar's disguise.

But endless lines of iambic pentameter can easily become sing-song, so Shakespeare uses a variety of devices to break up the pattern while still keeping a basic rhythm running. Usually the shifts from the regular pattern link in with the meaning or emotional pitch of the speech and serve to heighten it. In speeches where something is being explained or recounted there will be 'run-on' lines, where meaning runs over from one line to the next so seamlessly that there is no real break when they are spoken aloud. Speeches full of tortured emotion may have their lines broken up into two parts, which 'added together' may have more than the usual five stresses. Breaking up the flow of the language in this way suggests a character struggling with intense feelings and pain.

❂ Look at Act 4, scene 6, lines 160–9, Lear's impassioned attack on hypocrisy. Find examples of lines split into two parts. Read the speech aloud and try to hear the rhythm of stressed syllables. Identify the lines where you think there are more than five stresses.

Imagery

Imagery in *King Lear* is absolutely central to the text. It is not added on to highlight ideas already expressed. Images are used throughout to carry the meaning and sense of the story. The use of a style of language that is complex, intense and packed with images is central to the impact of the play.

Not all the characters have language equally rich in images. Goneril, Regan and Cornwall have very few images in their speeches because they are rational and unimaginative villains. They order, complain or plot: they do not greatly muse upon the world nor on issues beyond their own ambitions. Even Edmund uses relatively few images: he is a cold, calculating man of practical ideas. The greatness of his key speeches relies on the power of his logical arguments. Compare these 'camp of evil' characters to Lear, the Fool and (to a lesser extent) Kent, whose lines are full of images. These men are thinking beyond immediate events and actions and their imaginations throw up huge numbers of striking images to convey their complex thoughts.

It is important to identify a number of types of images that recur throughout the play and link to particular themes. They knit the complex issues of the play together with imaginative and vivid language. The main types to look for are:

• animals;
• references to splitting and cracking;
• eyes and sight;
• clothing;
• disease and healing;
• nothingness.

ANIMALS

There are 133 references to 64 different animals in the play! Most of the images refer to the cruelty of animals: to teeth, fangs, claws and beaks: the creature's tools for attack. Most of these references are made when Goneril and Regan are compared to animals in their viciousness. ✪ What is the dramatic purpose of comparing the sisters to animals?

SPLITTING AND CRACKING

There are many references to things (and people) breaking, splitting, cracking and shattering throughout the play. They are framed within the bigger thematic breaking apart of the kingdom by Lear, and by his and Gloucester's shattering of their families.

In a play with so much dislocation of order and consequent suffering, it is appropriate that hearts should break: Lear's, *but this heart/ Shall break into a hundred thousand flaws* (Act 2, scene 4, lines 279–80), and Gloucester's, *O! Madam, my old heart is crack'd, it's crack'd* (Act 2, scene 1, line 89). And Edgar, reporting Gloucester's death, says:

> *But his flawed heart,*
> *Alack, too weak the conflict to support,*
> *'Twixt two extremes of passion, joy and grief*
> *Burst smilingly.* (Act 5, scene 3, lines 194–7)

The now rarely used term *body politic* describes a nation or kingdom as a body. Lear's madness can be interpreted as a symbol for the state of his fractured or 'deranged' kingdom.

EYES AND SIGHT

Seeing and blindness, light and darkness: these contrasts recur throughout the play. It starts in the very first scene. Goneril says (line 56) she loves her father *Dearer than eyesight*. Kent, appalled at Lear's poor judgement, says *See better, Lear* (line 158).

Lear's near blindness in the chaos of the stormy night, and Gloucester's actual blinding, are both literal instances of sightlessness which are also symbolic of both men's inability to 'see' or understand the true nature of things. Shortly after his blinding Gloucester says, *I have no way, and therefore want no eyes* (Act 4, scene 1, line 18). He then opens this view of his own misery into a wider frame with a further blindness image when he says *'Tis the time's plague when madmen lead the blind* (line 46). He must stumble, lost in darkness, and sees in this a symbol for the trouble that the whole kingdom is suffering.

CLOTHING

The importance of clothing, and images referring to clothing, should remind us that *King Lear* is a stage play both seen and heard, and that the use of costume is a vital part of a successful production. Edgar and Kent's disguises are achieved by altering appearance: though Edgar puts on an assumed voice, Kent does not apparently change his plain speech very much. His disguise is purely visual. The Fool only ever appears in motley, the standard uniform of the court fool or jester.

But it is Lear's changes of clothes that are the most significant. He begins the play finely dressed, as befits a king. He is reduced to a soaked and dishevelled state by the storm, then tries to throw off even these sodden, soiled clothes to imitate Poor Tom's nakedness. His being given fresh clothes in Act 4, scene 7, when he has (temporarily) regained his sanity, provides a visual image symbolizing his inner, recovered, state.

Much of the tragedy in the play is the result of people believing false appearances. Clothing can be used in Lear's world to signify power and status or poverty and degradation. Often the finely dressed (Goneril, Regan and Edmund) are the most vicious and dangerous, while those forced to wear rags (Kent and Edgar) do good. When Lear begins to see the world for what it really is he cries, *Off, off, you lendings* (Act 3, scene 4, line 105) and tries to tear off the clothes that remind him of his lost kingship. He has perhaps heeded and is acting upon one of the most telling lines in the play, uttered a while before by Poor Tom: *set not thy sweet heart on proud array* (Act 3, scene 4, line 79). And this line of Tom's echoes Lear's earlier comment in Act 2, scene 4, to Regan:

> *If only to go warm were gorgeous,*
> *Why, nature needs not what thou gorgeous wear'st,*
> *Which scarcely keeps thee warm.* (lines 263–5)

DISEASE AND HEALING

Disease images occur intermittently through the play. When Kent and Lear quarrel in Act 1, scene 1, Kent cries *kill thy physician, and thy fee bestow/ Upon the foul disease* (lines 164–5). (Some versions of the play have a stage direction just before these lines indicating that Lear reaches for his sword, presumably thinking to strike or even *kill* Kent.)

The idea that Lear's suffering is a disease, caused by and embodied in Goneril, makes him complain to her that she is

> *a disease that's in my flesh,*
> *Which I must needs call mine: thou art a boil,*
> *A plague sore, an embossed carbuncle,*
> *In my corrupted blood.* (Act 2, scene 4, lines 217–20)

The fact that (in most editions of the play) a doctor is attending upon the recovering Lear at Cordelia's camp in Act 4, scene 7, is a symbolic image of disease and recovery. (Note that some versions of the play have the doctor's lines spoken by the Gentleman, probably for the practical purpose of simplifying the number of characters.) Cordelia takes up the theme of disease and recovery when she says, before kissing her father, *restoration hangs/ Thy medicine on my lips* (Act 4, scene 7, lines 26–7).

Another perspective on the disease imagery in the play is that, as in other Shakespeare tragedies, the disease of the king represents the sickness of the state.

NOTHINGNESS

LEAR: *what can you say to draw*
        A third more opulent than your sisters? Speak.
CORDELIA: *Nothing, my lord.*
LEAR: *Nothing?*
CORDELIA: *Nothing.*
LEAR: *Nothing will come of nothing.*
        (Act 1, scene 1, lines 85–90)

This curt exchange between Lear and Cordelia contrasts bleakly with the flowing poetry that surrounds it in Act 1, scene 1. Imagery of nothing and nothingness is central to the feeling of pessimism in the play. There is a stark division, especially in the first three Acts, between those who are acquiring material wealth and power (Goneril, Regan and Edmund) and those (Lear, Gloucester, Edgar and Kent) who have status and possessions stripped from them.

But more important than this type of loss is loss of identity. The Fool tells Lear, *Now thou art an O without a figure ... thou art nothing* (Act 1, scene 4, lines 188–90). Edgar endures loss of personality when he assumes the disguise of Poor Tom, saying, *Edgar I nothing am* (Act 2, scene 3, line 21).

○ Draw two Mini Mind Maps, one for eyes and sight and one for clothing images, showing how examples of these types of imagery work to achieve different effects in the play. Put references along the branches of your Map to show where key images are used.

Structure

Like Shakespeare's other great tragedies, such as *Hamlet*, *Othello* and *Macbeth*, the story of *King Lear* unfolds over five Acts. It is one of Shakespeare's longest plays.

To understand how the plot of the play is structured it is best to see the story as essentially the 'journeys' of two men, Lear principally, but with Gloucester's story as a major subplot closely paralleling Lear's journey. Try to understand the play like this rather than seeing each scene as a sequence of events involving all the large cast equally. There is so much happening in the play that it is easy to get lost and you must always remember that the story of King Lear himself is the core around which everything else ultimately operates.

Because the play is driven by the journeys that Lear and Gloucester make, more notes about the structure of the play are found in the 'Characterization' section of this guide, especially in the sections dealing with these two characters.

There will now be a short interval

? Imagine you were directing *King Lear* for a theatre.
Where would you put the interval, and why?
Remember this is the point where the audience gets a
break to talk about what they have seen and what
they think will happen.

Now take a short interval yourself.

OMMENTARY

Act 1, scene 1

◆ Gloucester introduces his illegitimate son Edmund to Kent.
◆ Lear announces his plan to rid himself of the responsibilities of ruling the kingdom by dividing it among his three daughters. He will use a love test to decide the portion each daughter receives.
◆ Cordelia refuses to join in the 'test of love' and is disinherited and banished.
◆ Kent is also banished for warning Lear that he is acting foolishly.
◆ Goneril and Regan are given half the kingdom each.

The play is dramatically 'kick-started' by this long, event-packed scene in which most of the main characters are introduced. Within a few pages Lear's fateful decision to divide the kingdom, from which the whole play develops, is enacted.

Kent and Gloucester talk of rumours about Lear's intentions towards his two sons-in-law, the Duke of Albany, who is married to Goneril, and the Duke of Cornwall who is Regan's husband. Cordelia, the youngest daughter and Lear's favourite, is unmarried, but two suitors, the Duke of Burgundy and the King of France, are at court to ask for her hand. Gloucester introduces Edmund, his illegitimate son, to Kent, and tells Kent that he loves Edmund as much as his legitimate son, Edgar. Gloucester makes light of the fact that he fathered an illegitimate child.

Lear enters with his three daughters. He tells the court that he has decided to hand over the rule of the kingdom to his daughters. The share each daughter will receive depends on how much they say they love him.

Goneril speaks first, saying her father is *dearer than eyesight, space, and liberty* to her (line 56). Then it is Regan's turn. She claims: *I am alone felicitate/ In your dear Highnesses love* (lines 75–6). But Lear's favourite daughter, Cordelia, refuses to take part in the test. She will say only that she loves him as duty instructs a daughter to love a father, not more or less.

When Cordelia refuses to declare her love more extravagantly Lear flies into a rage. He disowns her and announces that Goneril and Regan will inherit half the kingdom each. He calls the two men who seek Cordelia's hand in marriage and asks if they will take her with no dowry. The King of France accepts her and leads her off to live with him in France. Notice the irony in Cordelia, who is to become a model of virtue and obedience later in the play, being the first of the daughters to rebel against Lear's will.

Kent tries to intervene to warn Lear that he is acting rashly. He is torn between respect for the king and anger at what is happening. He veers between calling Lear *my lord* and *old man*. He too is banished. Lear then calls forward Albany and Cornwall and gives them powers over the kingdom he has just split between their two wives. Lear now plans to live with each daughter in turn, keeping a retinue of one hundred knights who will travel and lodge with him. He is concerned to keep up the appearance and privileges of a king.

The only time Cordelia addresses her sisters directly in the whole play is when she is leaving with the King of France. Ominously she says

> I know what you are;
> And like a sister am most loath to call
> Your faults as they are named. (lines 269–71)

A key theme in *King Lear* is family and what happens when family order and duty breaks down. Lear has broken his family apart and this will threaten the stability of the larger 'family' of the kingdom. There is already a sense that what Lear has done will have terrible consequences. Only Lear seems unaware of this. Notice how he never asks any of his daughters how they might rule the kingdom, nor does he offer them any practical advice. He is acting with the arrogance and power of a king, but without showing any judgement.

The scene ends as it began: two figures on stage talking quietly. Goneril and Regan discuss Lear's behaviour. They feel he is acting in wild and unpredictable ways, and though it has benefited them today they are united in believing that even without retaining the power to rule his kingdom, their father could threaten them in the future. He might turn against them as he did Cordelia.

Brainstorm a Mini Mind Map of key themes and ideas that are presented to the audience in this long first scene.

Act 1, scene 2

◆ Edmund reveals his ambitions and plans.
◆ He begins to convince Gloucester that Edgar is planning to kill the old man. He presents the forged letter.
◆ He convinces Edgar that his father is angry with him. Edgar readily accepts Edmund's help and advice.

The struggle within Gloucester's family is a subplot mirroring the main parent/child dispute between Lear and his daughters. Notice how Shakespeare balances the 'stage presence' of the opening moves of each plot line:

• Act 1, scene 1, with all its characters and events, is 309 lines long.
• Act 1, scene 2, given over entirely to Edmund presenting himself to the audience via two powerful soliloquies and the first moves in his plot against Edgar, is just over 180 lines: almost two-thirds that of the opening scene of the main plot.

This indicates how important Edmund is to the structure of *King Lear*.

Edmund's explosive opening speech (lines 1–22) contrasts dramatically with his reticence in the presence of his father and Kent in Act 1, scene 1. Read the speech aloud to hear the full force of the poetry in which Edmund frames his ideas.

Edmund refuses to accept the rules of society that place him, as a bastard, below his legitimate brother. He says that *nature* is his goddess. This introduces a theme that runs throughout the play: nature, often the cruel harsh face of nature, conflicting with human society and order. Edmund claims his qualities are equal to Edgar's. Notice the number of rhetorical questions he asks, all designed to draw the audience into his argument. He is full of energy and confidence.

By contrast his father seems to have lost the lewd good humour he displayed when speaking to Kent in scene 1. He enters muttering about what has happened at court. Gloucester falls instantly into the trap Edmund sets with the forged letter and believes that it is from Edgar. The letter appears to be proposing that he and Edmund plan a conspiracy against their father and divide the estate equally (as Goneril and Regan have each inherited half the kingdom). Edmund makes a show of defending his brother, but offers deliberately lame excuses as to why the forged letter might exist: *I hope, for my brother's justification, he wrote this but as an essay, or taste of my virtue* (lines 44–5). Edmund knows there is nothing in this to persuade Gloucester that the letter is anything but a true revelation of Edgar's unnatural and murderous feelings towards his father.

Edmund weaves another strand into his plot when he claims that he has heard Edgar say many times that *sons at perfect age and fathers declined, the father should be as ward to the son and the son manage his revenue* (lines 73–5).

Gloucester issues orders that Edgar be found and detained. Edmund suggests that Gloucester should not act until he has heard Edgar actually condemn himself. Gloucester agrees. Edmund is already controlling Gloucester, who appears to be both appallingly gullible (unable to recognize either Edmund's or Edgar's handwriting?) and weak. He falls into a superstitious lament about bad omens and recent solar eclipses. (This is also a 'hook' used by Shakespeare to draw in his audiences. Around the time the play was first performed there were solar eclipses which many people believed to be bad signs.) Following Edmund's powerful proclamations, Gloucester's flight from reason into superstition seems the refuge of an old and already defeated man.

Gloucester exits and Edmund surges into another forceful speech to the audience, ridiculing and destroying the views of superstitious people such as his father. Every man is responsible for his own actions. A man who tries to excuse his evil actions by saying he was born under bad stars is guilty of *admirable evasion ... to lay his goatish disposition on the charge of a star* (lines 126–8).

Edgar enters. Edmund's quoting the prediction he claims to have read (lines 142–8) is a piece of pure mischief-making, showing us how much he enjoys playing the villain. He tells Edgar he has offended their father and that Edgar better keep out of Gloucester's way. Edmund acts the concerned sibling beautifully, suggesting that Edgar take refuge at his lodging.

Edgar, perhaps exhibiting a gullibility he has inherited from his father, falls into the plan, hardly pausing to think what it is that he may have done to cause such parental rage (the supposed offence is never made clear). One easily agrees with Edmund when he calls his father *credulous* (line 175) and his brother noble with a nature *so far from doing harms/ That he suspects none* (lines 176–7). Such trust is not something that a villain like Edmund would see as a worthy quality. But it is important to understand that Jacobean audiences would have been familiar with a tradition that presented good characters as easily fooled because their honesty was such that they never imagined the scheming deceits of villains.

Act 1, scene 3

◆ Goneril complains to her steward Oswald about the behaviour of Lear and his followers.
◆ She encourages Oswald to be less respectful towards Lear.

A short period of time has elapsed since the division of the kingdom. Lear and his knights are lodged with Goneril and Albany. We do not know if the knights are actually causing as much uproar as Goneril claims or if she is using them as a way of beginning to provoke Lear. But we do learn that Lear has hit one of Goneril's 'gentlemen' for *chiding of the Fool*. Lear cares for his Fool and is prepared to defend him. Lear still displays a violent temper.

Goneril instructs her steward Oswald to *Put on what weary negligence you please* (line 13) towards Lear. She will answer for the consequences. Already we can see the balance of power beginning to shift from Lear to his daughter. Remember that as a host, Goneril had a traditional duty to behave graciously towards her guest.

Act 1, scene 4

◆ Kent appears before Lear in disguise and asks to serve him.
◆ Oswald's disrespect infuriates Lear. Oswald is tripped and ridiculed by Kent.
◆ The Fool begins taunting Lear for causing this lack of respect by his own actions.

◆ Lear and Goneril row. She wants Lear to reduce his train of knights.

◆ In a fury Lear decides to move to Regan's house. Albany, arriving late to the row, is shocked by Lear's rage.

Lear returns to Goneril's house from hunting to find Kent disguised as a plain serving gentleman seeking employment. With typical honesty and bluntness (so typical of the real Kent one wonders why Lear does not suspect!), Kent styles himself as one who

Can keep honest counsel, ride, run, mar a curious
Tale in the telling and deliver a plain message bluntly.
(lines 32–3)

This is a perfect description of Kent's character. Lear agrees to take him on. Oswald is doing as Goneril ordered, wandering off without properly answering Lear. Lear is still acting with kingly arrogance, and is angry at the sudden lack of respect shown by Goneril's household. Oswald returns but refuses to recognize Lear as the king, saying instead that he is merely *my lady's father* (line 78). Lear strikes Oswald (further evidence of a violent temper) and Kent joins in by tripping Oswald. This sets Kent firmly in Lear's good books.

The Fool makes his first appearance. He taunts Lear for what he has done. He speaks a lot about property and the fact that Lear has given his away, implying that he has given the right to respect away with it. The Fool's attacks unsettle Lear because they underline the lack of respect that has already angered him. Lear begins to question his own identity (lines 222–6). Loss of identity is a key theme in the play, especially for Lear, and is introduced here.

Goneril complains about the uproar Lear's knights are causing and demands he reduce his train (and thereby the visible sign of his power as a king) by fifty men. If he will not do this, she says she will. Lear threatens to gather his men and go to Regan's. This may be a bluff, but Goneril is determined to have her way. Albany enters and is distressed to see the angry scene and Lear's discomfort. Lear vents his anger on Goneril in a powerful speech where he wishes that she will either be sterile or produce children who *Turn all her mother's pains and benefits/ To laughter and contempt* (lines 283–4).

Lear is not only angry, but upset: *I am ashamed/ That thou has power to shake my manhood thus* (lines 293–4). He is showing the first signs of weakness. He exits, Goneril clearly having got the better of him. Albany is shocked but Goneril is icily calm and controlled. Lear returns briefly to report that fifty of his men have already been dismissed (although later in the play there are references to a hundred still being present).

Goneril explains to her husband that such a powerful body of followers *hold our lives at mercy* (line 324). Albany fails to assert himself. Goneril sends Oswald to Regan with a letter *to inform her of my particular fear* (line 334), to tell her what has happened. She encourages Oswald to add anything he wishes. She clearly trusts Oswald as a co-conspirator and not merely a servant.

Act 1, scene 5

◆ Lear sends Kent to Regan with a letter announcing his arrival. Lear begins to feel he may be going mad.

Lear sends Kent to Regan to announce his arrival. Kent must not tell Regan about the confrontation with Goneril. The Fool maintains his chorus of taunts about Lear's predicament. Lear admits for the first time that he has wronged Cordelia. He wonders if the guilt of what he has done might drive him mad. But he still thinks all the problems are the result of ungrateful children, not his own folly. This small scene is a pivotal point in the plot. Lear's sufferings are really beginning.

Get in on the act

? In Act 1, scene 1, Gloucester refers to Edmund (a grown man remember) as *this knave* who *came saucily into the world* (line 20) and tells Kent there *was good sport at his making* (line 22). What do these remarks suggest about Gloucester's character? What might Edmund feel hearing them? Edmund's polite reserve in this scene contrasts dramatically with his speeches in Act 1, scene 2. Why is he so quiet in scene 1?

? Draw a Mini Mind Map of the qualities of character Shakespeare is establishing for Cordelia in this opening scene?

? What dangers can you see in Lear giving up actual authority but being keen to maintain the appearance of a great king? What does his desire tell us about Lear's character? Write a brief character study of Lear based on what you learn in the first scene.

? On the evidence of how Lear behaves in this Act, what sort of ruler do you think he might have been? (Look also at Goneril and Regan's conversation in Act 1, scene 1, lines 288–306.) Add your ideas to the character study.

? Given that we later see just how much Cordelia loves and honours her father, what reasons can she have for answering in such a cold way in the love test (Act 1, scene1)?

Test your knowledge

Beside these quotes from Act 1 put (1) the names of the speakers, (2) who they are speaking to, or what about.

1 *Though this knave came something saucily to the world, before he was sent for ...*
2 *Sir, I love you more than word can wield the matter.*
3 *I love your majesty/ According to my bond, no more nor less.*
4 *Since that respect and fortunes are his love,/ I shall not be his wife.*
5 *It is his hand, my lord; but I hope his heart is not in the contents.*
6 *By day and night he wrongs me; every hour/ He flashes into one gross crime or other.*
7 *Why came not the slave back to me when I called him?*
8 *And from her derogate body never spring/ A babe to honour her.*
9 *He may enguard his dotage with their powers/ And hold our lives in mercy.*
10 *Thou shouldst not have been old till thou hadst been wise.*
(Answers, see p. 90)

... But you can be young and wise, if you take a break now.

Act 2, scene 1

◆ Edmund learns that conflict between Albany and Cornwall is likely.

◆ Edmund persuades Edgar to flee, wounds himself and tells Gloucester that Edgar attacked him.

◆ Gloucester, believing Edgar to be plotting his murder, orders that he be hunted down.

◆ Regan and Cornwall arrive at Gloucester's castle.

◆ Edmund promises to serve Cornwall.

Gloucester's castle. Edmund learns that Regan and Cornwall are expected. Unlike Goneril, who confronted Lear face to face, Regan is leaving home to avoid her father. We learn that conflict (*likely wars*, line 10) between Albany and Cornwall is threatening.

Edmund uses all this information to his advantage. He calls Edgar from his hiding place and asks him if he has spoken out against Cornwall and Regan. He makes Edgar's position appear more dangerous by suggesting that they too are angry with him. Edgar now seems a little less gullible, beginning to suspect a conspiracy against him. After the mock fight between the brothers Edmund deliberately inflicts a small wound on himself. Edmund paints a very black, false picture of Edgar to Gloucester, saying that the fight developed because Edgar tried to involve him in the plot against their father.

Gloucester is appalled by what he sees as a terrible breaking of natural family bonds. He vows that Edgar will be hunted down and executed. Anyone aiding Edgar will die. Note the parallel between Gloucester's readiness to condemn a son to death purely on the word of another with Lear's disowning of Cordelia for not saying she loved him with sufficient enthusiasm. Both old men are reacting with fury but little judgement. The punishments they inflict or seek to inflict are extreme. Both appear capable of 'unnatural' degrees of violence towards their children. The breaking of family bonds and duties can be seen as a two-way route in the play: children should respect their parents; equally parents should never wish harm on their children. Goneril, Regan and Edmund are perhaps just more efficient villains than their old fathers.

Regan and Cornwall arrive. Like Lear, Gloucester uses disowning as a means of revenge. He will disown Edgar in favour of Edmund, who is *a loyal and natural boy* (line 83). *Natural* has an ironic double meaning here. Edmund is a bastard, conceived *saucily* outside of marriage and therefore perhaps a more natural offspring than children born conventionally within families. But in the modern, derogatory sense of the word Edmund behaves like a bastard, especially towards his father. In this he is most unnatural.

Regan says she has no intention of being a host to Lear or his train of troublesome knights, which is why she has come to Gloucester's castle. Edmund offers his duty and services to Cornwall. The two men, the key male villains of the play, are easily drawn together.

This scene shows the evil characters gaining ground. Edmund's plot against Edgar is working. Cornwall and Edmund readily form an alliance. Edmund now displays almost total command over Gloucester. He turns the arrival of Cornwall to his advantage, though we do not yet know how he will use the alliance. Regan and Cornwall appear to be in charge of events at the castle. Lear is diminished by the loss of his knights. Gloucester is beginning to look powerless in his own home.

○ How are the two plots (Lear's family and Gloucester's) coming together in this scene?

Act 2, scene 2

◆ Kent, acting as Lear's messenger, quarrels with Oswald, Goneril's messenger.
◆ Cornwall puts Kent in the stocks for beating Oswald.
◆ Kent reveals he has a letter from Cordelia.

Kent and Oswald meet outside Gloucester's castle. Kent forces a quarrel with Oswald, who won't rise to the challenge of Kent's blunt but wonderfully extravagant insults (especially his 'list', lines 13–22). Oswald cannot understand Kent's unprovoked aggression. When Kent challenges him to draw his sword, Oswald cries for help, revealing himself to be a coward. ○ Why do you think Kent picks the fight with Oswald?

Edmund, Goneril, Regan and Cornwall come running. Cornwall stops Kent, who is beating Oswald. Kent presents no real justification for his attack, but stresses his commitment to plain speaking. His blunt manner shows he has little respect for Cornwall:

> *Sir, 'tis my occupation to be plain:*
> *I have seen better faces in my time*
> *Than stands on any shoulder that I see*
> *Before me at this instant.* (lines 90–4)

Cornwall orders Kent to be put in the stocks. Kent says that he is on the King's business and should be treated with more respect. Cornwall ignores him. Kent is to stay in the stocks until noon, but Regan, with chilling malice, insists he be left all night. This is typical of Regan, to add a vicious twist to violence that others begin. She is both sadistic and cowardly.

❂ What other key scene shows Regan acting in this way?

Gloucester pleads Kent's case but is ignored. He stays with Kent when the others exit to offer his sympathies. Kent is stoical: his easy acceptance of his punishment makes him seem to rise above the others in this scene, even though he has been guilty of an unprovoked attack. We sense that Kent is right even when acting wrongly, and approve of him exposing Oswald's cowardliness. Kent reveals he is carrying a letter from Cordelia in which she vows to redress the wrongs that have happened since she was banished.

In a scene where the forces of evil appear to be unstoppably gaining ground, Cordelia's letter brings a faint glimmer of hope for the future.

Act 2, scene 3

◆ Edgar, on the run, disguises himself as 'Poor Tom'.

Edgar is a fugitive, alone in the countryside. The towns and seaports are watched, his father's men are searching for him. He decides to disguise himself as a 'bedlam beggar', an itinerant madman. Such figures would have been familiar objects of pity or amusement to Jacobean audiences. He describes how he will effect this disguise:

my face I'll grime with filth,
Blanket my loins, elf all my hair in knots. (lines 9–10)

That the son of an earl is reduced to this reveals the seriousness of Edgar's plight. It is a vivid example of goodness overwhelmed by evil. And the disguise Edgar describes is a terrible foreshadowing of what will happen to Lear.

Act 2, scene 4

◆ Lear arrives at Gloucester's castle and finds Kent in the stocks.
◆ Goneril arrives. Lear complains to his daughters. They further reduce his train of knights.
◆ Driven to fury by their ingratitude, Lear rushes out into the storm. Regan has the doors locked against his return.

Lear arrives at Gloucester's castle, and is upset (note, not driven to fury as he would have been before) to see his messenger in the stocks. Lear cannot believe Regan and Cornwall are responsible for *shaming* his servant.

✪ What might Lear's use of the word 'shaming' reveal about his thinking?

The Fool continues to mock Lear, picking on the theme of parents and children. Lear pays little attention. He is becoming obsessed with his own mental state, thinking he may go mad with grief at what is happening to him at the hands of his daughters. Regan has not come out to greet him. He goes off to look for her. Compare this to Act 2, scene 1, when Lear automatically sends a man he has on hand to bring back Oswald. Lear's power to command is rapidly waning. The Fool underlines Lear's plight by a rhyme (lines 74–81) which warns against following a master whose power is failing. But the Fool will not obey his own advice.

Lear is more angry and upset when he returns. Regan and Cornwall say they are tired and will not speak with him. Lear senses a trick and sends Gloucester to get a better answer. The Fool, never one to miss a chance to criticize Lear's behaviour, mocks him when the king says that maybe his son-in-law is actually too tired to see him. The Fool gives two examples of absurd kindness. ✪ Can you find and explain them?

Cornwall and Regan enter. Kent is freed. Lear is distressed and weak. Instead of offering support and sympathy, Regan coldly suggests that Lear should let others command him. He should return to Goneril and beg her pardon. Lear is astonished. He thought he was travelling to a sanctuary, the last he had. He is reduced to pleading:

> *Dear daughter, I confess that I am old;*
> *Age is unnecessary: on my knees I beg*
> *That you'll vouchsafe me raiment, bed and food.*
>   (lines 149–51)

Goneril arrives. With her sister present, Regan becomes more bold in her attacks on Lear. She says he must go back to Goneril with fifty, not a hundred, knights. Then she suggests a further reduction in his train. Lear fears he is losing his mind. He curses Goneril but has not yet attacked Regan. ☉ How does Goneril's arrival shift the dramatic development of this scene?

This is a pivotal moment in the plot. Power has entirely slipped from Lear's hands. The storm begins. Tension has been rising throughout the scene. Now the pressure is released when, unable to make his daughters see things his way, Lear rushes out into the wild night. Gloucester follows Lear and returns saying that the king is in *high rage*. He describes the bleak heath into which Lear has fled. The storm is rising and there is little shelter. Gloucester appeals to Cornwall and Regan in the same way that Lear was reduced to doing. Gloucester's power has slipped to almost nothing in this scene. Regan characteristically adds a little touch of cruelty, ordering the doors to be locked.

Lear's shifting position structures this scene. As he becomes more and more aware of his powerlessness, his mental instability grows. Yet he knows what is happening to him. Lear is that most tragic of figures: a man going mad who knows he is losing his reason.

Think about

? How does the 'power' of Kent in Act 2, scene 2, contrast with that exercised by Cornwall and Regan?

> ? Why has Shakespeare given plain-speaking Kent such extravagant and imaginative insults in this scene? What dramatic purpose do they serve?
>
> ? How is the storm symbolic of what is happening at the end of this Act?

Test your knowledge

1 Who inflicts a wound on his own arm. Why?
2 Who bars *all ports* so that *the villain shall not 'scape*? And who is the villain?
3 Till when does Cornwall want Kent to stay in the stocks, and how long does Regan suggest his punishment be extended?
4 Where does Edmund first hide to escape *the hunt*?
5 Who has to beg on bended knee for *raiment, bed and food*?
6 Whose *young bones* does Lear want to be struck *with lameness*?
7 In Act 2, scene 4, how many followers does Regan entreat Lear to bring with him?
8 Who *are in the poorest things superfluous*?
9 In Act 2, scene 4, what prompts Cornwall to suggest that they withdraw into the castle?
10 By the end of Act 2, scene 4, how many followers does Regan say Lear can have?

(Answers, see p. 90)

At the end of Act 2, events are picking up speed. But you should take a break now.

Act 3, scene 1

◆ Kent and the Gentleman search for Lear on the heath. Kent asks the Gentleman to deliver a ring and letters to Cordelia.

Some hours have passed since Lear rushed from Gloucester's castle. Lear is somewhere out in the storm with only the Fool for company.

The Gentleman's account provides a vivid picture of Lear's now apparently complete madness. He stresses the powerlessness of Lear against the storm, saying how he *strives in his little world of man to out-storm/ The to and fro conflicting wind and rain* (lines 10–11). One underlying theme of the play is the helplessness of man against the forces of nature, vividly brought to life in the Gentleman's description.

Kent speaks of the division between Albany and Cornwall, suggesting troubles to come. France plans to invade England. French forces are already camped on English soil at Dover. Cordelia is with them. Kent, ever the loyal and practical servant, gives the Gentleman a ring (as a mark of identification) and asks him to deliver it to her.

This short scene brings the audience 'up to speed' with events that we don't actually see. It sets the tone for Act 3 which is composed of seven short, sharp scenes.

Act 3, scene 2

◆ Lear, driven to madness, raves in the storm.
◆ The Fool and Kent try to persuade him to shelter in a hovel.

Both Lear and Gloucester are spiralling downwards to their dooms throughout this Act. As the storm rages, so does Lear, with two extravagant and passionate speeches to open the scene. Study these carefully. Lear may be raving like a madman, but there is a logic to the poetry in which he speaks of the things that have driven him to madness. ❂ How does the Fool react to Lear's madness at this point?

Kent catches up with them. His view of the storm is more practical: he thinks it unlikely that a man as frail as Lear will be able to survive it. But Lear appears to be little affected by the cold and rain. He sees the storm as anger from the gods at man's evils (lines 49–59). The wild night is symbolic of judgement and reckoning for sinners. But he sees himself as a victim, *more sinned against than sinning* (line 59).

Kent tries to persuade Lear and the Fool to take shelter. Lear seems totally preoccupied with his own whirling thoughts until he notices the physical suffering of the loyal Fool. There is a compassion in Lear that we have not seen before. Lear agrees to be led to a hovel.

Left alone briefly, the Fool delivers a *prophecy* to the audience (lines 80–95). He lists the sins and sinners of the world he lives in, then imagines a time when Albion (Britain) will be a kind of utopia where these evils will not exist, *where slanders do not live in tongues,/ Nor cut purses come not to throngs* (lines 89–90).

It is interesting to notice the last line of the speech, which may have been used as a bit of scene-setting by Shakespeare for his audience. The Fool concludes his vision by saying *This prophecy Merlin shall make, for I live before his time* (line 95). The setting of the play is England, and such small descriptions of the kingdom and wider society as are provided suggest a world pretty much like the one that Shakespeare lived in. But the play is supposedly set much, much earlier. Holinshed, one of Shakespeare's main sources, locates the story as happening in the eighth century BC. Merlin, the magician in the legends of King Arthur, is said by Holinshed to have lived in the sixth century BC.

Whether or not the Jacobean audience thought Lear was a real king back in antiquity, or whether they realized the play was based on a legend with no real historical base, they probably knew about the much more popular Arthurian legends. By having the Fool say he is living before Merlin, Shakespeare has a way of reminding the audience that the story they are watching supposedly happened a very long time ago.

❂ If Shakespeare had wanted historical accuracy, he would have had to create a much simpler and cruder world for his play. Might there be a deliberate purpose in making the story take place in a world that resembled the one his audience actually lived in? What power does this lend to the play?

Act 3, scene 3

◆ Gloucester decides he has to help his king.
◆ He tells Edmund, who decides to betray Gloucester to Cornwall.

Gloucester opens this scene by confessing to Edmund his desire to help the king. He has been warned *neither to speak of him, entreat for him, or any way sustain him* (lines 4–5). This shows not only how far Gloucester has been diminished, but also how Goneril, Regan and Cornwall have turned completely against Lear.

Gloucester reveals that Albany is set to clash with Cornwall. He repeats the story we first heard in Act 3, scene 1, of the arrival of French forces at Dover. He suggests that Edmund must help him help Lear. Edmund, again displaying his ability to turn events instantly to his own evil purposes, decides to betray his father to Cornwall.

Act 3, scene 4

◆ Lear, Kent and the Fool reach the hovel, but Lear continues to rave out on the stormy heath.
◆ They find 'Poor Tom' (Edgar) in the hovel. In Tom's company, Lear begins to associate himself with the poor and homeless.
◆ Gloucester finds Lear and the others. He reports that Goneril and Regan want Lear dead.

This is a dark and chilling scene, in many ways at the spiritual low point of the play. The evil characters are gathered together, united and secure in Gloucester's castle. Lear, Kent, the Fool and (for a time) Gloucester are out in the pitiless night. Shakespeare has created tremendous contrasts of symbols: light and dark, warmth and cold, the calculated planning of Goneril and Regan driving the madness of Lear and the despair of Gloucester.

Lear will not follow the Fool into the hovel. He says that the harm the storm does him is nothing compared to his inner torment. Lear underlines the symbolism of the storm in the world reflecting the whirling madness in his soul. He returns to the ingratitude of his daughters, and wants to stay out in the storm and pray. ✪ For what does Lear pray? How does this suggest a change in his character?

Lear's own suffering and madness is bringing him to a new compassion and concern for the world.

The Fool rushes from the hovel, terrified by a spirit inside. Kent kindly takes the frightened Fool's hand. The

Fool has been shown as a nervous and rather frail figure during the storm, which contrasts rather with his earlier cutting wit and taunts. Kent calls the 'spirit' out. It is Edgar disguised as 'Poor Tom'.

Lear recognizes himself in Tom, and is convinced that Tom must have been driven mad by cruel daughters. Edgar, as Tom, falls into a manner of talking and ranting that resembles, but is distinct from, Lear's mad utterances. Tom describes the *foul fiend* that hunts him, then creates a history for himself as a former *serving man, proud in heart and mind* (line 82) who fell into degenerate ways: *Wine loved I deeply, dice dearly, and in woman, out-paramoured the Turk* (lines 87–8). We can read in Edgar's account a comment on Oswald.

Tom acts as a powerful catalyst on Lear, who seizes on Tom's story and his present plight as evidence of the cruelty of the world. In Tom, he believes he sees humanity in its essence, literally in its naked form. Lear develops a kind of twisted admiration for Tom. He tries to tear off his clothes to imitate Tom's nakedness.

During this confusion Gloucester arrives. Lear's decline and Gloucester's are bound together when Gloucester says:

Thou sayest the King grows mad: I'll tell thee, friend,
I am almost mad myself. I had a son
Now outlawed from my blood, he sought my life. (lines 158–60)

Perhaps because he fears that his father might see through the disguise, Tom's ravings become more extreme. Lear is convinced that Tom is actually a learned philosopher and asks him questions about the nature of the world. Gloucester has prepared shelter in an outhouse of his castle.

Edgar launches into a fictional account of his years of wandering as a despised mad beggar. Lear's concern for Tom shows that he is developing a sympathy for, and an association with, the poor and excluded of the world. He is learning pity, not just for himself, but for all mankind. When they finally agree to go to Gloucester's shelter, Tom is part of the group.

❂ What is the dramatic significance of having Edgar/Poor Tom join the outcast group around the king at this point?

A scene in which one character is a Fool, two are disguised, one feigns madness and one is actually mad could be a dramatist's nightmare. But Shakespeare fills this scene with the whirling speeches of madmen who speak wisdom, and with humanity and pathos. All the 'good' characters, apart from Cordelia, are struggling together against the storm and madness.

Act 3, scene 5

◆ Edmund tells Cornwall that Gloucester has tried to help Lear. Cornwall values Edmund as an ally.

Cornwall intends to punish Gloucester for aiding the king. Edmund is sent out to find his father. Edmund feigns being torn between obeying Cornwall and being loyal to his *blood* (line 22). Throughout this scene, there is a new ruthlessness in Cornwall's tone, and an assumed authority, as if he is the ruler in waiting.

Act 3, scene 6

◆ Lear conducts a 'trial' of his ungrateful daughters while he shelters in the outhouse.
◆ Gloucester brings a coach to take Lear to safety at Dover where Cordelia and the French army have set up camp.

Lear, Kent, the Fool and Poor Tom are led by Gloucester to the shelter he has prepared. He goes off to bring provisions to them.

Lear's madness consistently has method in it. He provides, through his madness, another way of looking at the world and what is happening to him which has a logic of its own. Nothing that he says is actually detached from reality.

He decides to judge his daughters in their absence. Tom and the Fool are made to sit on the bench and assist. He uses a stool to represent Goneril and accuses it of kicking him. He then imagines that Regan has escaped from the 'courtroom'.

This scene is not without some black humour. Shakespeare's audience might have drawn a wry parallel between a madman holding court to try invisible criminals, supported by another madman and a Fool, and the actual judges and courts of their day.

✪ It could be argued that this mock trial serves very little practical or logical purpose in the development of the plot. But what does it add to the development of characters involved?

This is the point at which the Fool vanishes from the play.

Gloucester returns. He knows that Goneril and Regan plan to murder Lear. He has prepared a coach (*litter*, line 88) to spirit Lear away to Dover and safety. This is the last scene featuring the Fool. His role has been largely taken over by Edgar in his Poor Tom disguise. His rather strange last line, *and I'll go to bed at noon* (line 84), may have been a light-hearted aside to the audience saying that he had no more work to do.

Act 3, scene 7

◆ Cornwall and Regan blind Gloucester as punishment for helping Lear.
◆ Cornwall is wounded by a servant who is appalled at the blinding of Gloucester.
◆ Regan orders Gloucester to be thrown out into the night.

The scene in the play that contains the greatest cruelty and physical shock begins with some mechanical plot development. Cornwall tells Goneril to return to Albany with a letter detailing the French invasion. He expects Albany to side with him. Edmund is sent to accompany Goneril: Cornwall expresses a twisted awareness of Edmund's possible sensitivity when he says *Edmund, keep you our sister company. The revenges we are bound to take upon your traitorous father are not fit for your beholding* (lines 6–9). Add to that the vicious cries of Goneril and Regan – *Hang him instantly!/ Pluck out his eyes!* (lines 4–5) and we are left in no doubt that Gloucester is doomed. Oswald brings news that Lear has escaped to Dover with thirty-six of his knights.

Bound to a chair and questioned by Goneril, Regan and Cornwall, Gloucester confesses that he helped Lear. When Gloucester calls down *winged Vengeance* upon Goneril and Regan (line 65), Cornwall gouges out one of Gloucester's eyes. The capital *V* suggests that Gloucester is referring not just to swift justice but to one of the mythical three Furies, probably Tisiphone, the Avenger of Blood.

○ Study the way Gloucester responds to his tormentors up to this point. Describe his tone. Why might he speak as he does?

Appalled by such horrors, one of Cornwall's trusted and long-serving servants begs him to stop this torture. There is a fight and Regan runs the servant through from behind, an act which underlines her unnatural actions and her cowardice. ✪ How do you react to her actions here? Cornwall has been wounded, but he finds the strength to put out Gloucester's other eye.

Regan taunts Gloucester, saying how Edmund hates him and conspires against him. In his sudden blindness, Gloucester 'sees' that he has been misled all along. Regan, seemingly revelling in the violence, has Gloucester thrown from his own castle saying *let him smell/ His way to Dover* (lines 92–3). She helps her wounded husband from the stage. Two loyal servants help Gloucester. They plan to take him to Poor Tom, who they hope will act as his guide.

At this point in the play evil seems to have triumphed in an appalling show of blood-letting. Directors usually have the interval at this point, and theatrical tradition has it that the interval break is a point where things begin to develop dramatically. But at the end of this Act the king is mad, Gloucester is blind, both are running for their lives. Only Cornwall's rather incidental wound from a servant gives any hint of the way the drama might swing.

Think about

?   What is the dramatic effect of having quick changes of scene throughout Act 3?

?   Imagine you were directing Act 3, scenes 2 and 4, the storm scenes, for the stage. How would you design them? What effects would you be aiming for to support the text? Write a brief account of your ideas.

?   The questioning of Gloucester in scene 7 can be contrasted to the 'trial' conducted by Lear in scene 6. What dramatic effects does the contrast provide?

?   How do you feel about the Fool disappearing from the story at the end of Act 3, scene 6? If he stayed on with Lear, what role might he fulfil?

Test your knowledge

1 What proof of his identity does Kent give the Gentleman to show Cordelia?
2 Who is *more sinned against than sinning*?
3 What *raineth every day*?
4 What is the *realm of Albion*?
5 Who is the spirit the Fool discovers in the hovel?
6 What was Poor Tom supposed to be before he became a mad beggar?
7 In Lear's imagination, what creatures are Trey, Blanch and Sweetheart?
8 How many knights follow Lear to Dover?
9 How does Regan kill the First Servant?
10 What 'first aid' do the servants plan to apply to Gloucester's eyes?

(Answers, see p. 90)

This is the point in the play when the interval usually occurs, so take a break now.

Act 4, scene 1

◆ Edgar, still disguised as Poor Tom, meets his blind father and begins leading him to Dover.

Edgar considers the virtues of being like the mad beggar he pretends to be. A beggar has no fear of falling any lower.

Gloucester is handed over to Tom by an old man. Gloucester is suffering terribly. He tells Tom how he wishes he could 'see' Edgar again to ask his forgiveness. The cruelty of the situation prompts Edgar to muse on the gods that rule men's lives:

As flies to wanton boys are we to the gods;
They kill us for their sport. (lines 36–7)

This bleak statement echoes the harsh view of the world that Lear has come to recognize. Gloucester, displaying kindness and consideration despite his agony, tells the old man to bring

Tom some clothes. Gloucester says it is fitting for the mad to lead the blind. The father and son of a noble family, brought down to such poverty and suffering, make a powerful image.

Gloucester, like Lear, muses on justice. He considers the role he believes the gods play in controlling men's lives. Like Lear, he begins to see that he has to be stripped of power and wealth in order to see the world for what it is. He adopts an almost Marxist view of the world, where *distribution should undo excess/ And each man have enough* (lines 69–70).

But these thoughts are overwhelmed by Gloucester's pain and desire to end his life. He offers Tom money if he will lead him to the cliff at Dover, implying that he plans to throw himself off.

✪ Draw a Mini Mind Map showing the similarities between Lear's changes through suffering and Gloucester's.

Act 4, scene 2

◆ Goneril and Edmund return to Albany's castle.
◆ Albany accuses Goneril of cruelty to her father. He is appalled at what has happened to Gloucester and at her part in it.
◆ They learn that Cornwall has died from his wound.

Goneril and Edmund have returned to Albany's castle. Goneril is surprised that Albany has not come out to greet her. Oswald describes Albany as *never a man so changed* (line 3). Albany is glad that the French have landed and is appalled by Edmund's treachery. Goneril sends Edmund to Cornwall to prepare for battle against the French. Before he goes, she begins her sexual advances towards him, saying she will be his mistress.

When Albany appears we see how much he has altered in the lengthy period that he has been absent from the stage. He stands up to his wife, calling her and Regan *tigers, not daughters* (line 40). She accuses him of being a *milk-livered man* (line 50). Albany says he would like to tear her limb from limb.

A messenger tells them that Cornwall is dead. The messenger also has a letter for Goneril from Regan. It is at this point that Goneril begins to turn on her sister. She is suspicious that the now-widowed Regan will court Edmund. Learning from the messenger the full horror of what has been done to Gloucester, Albany vows:

> I live
> To thank thee for the love thou showd'st the King,
> And to revenge thine eyes. (lines 93–5)

✪ Do you think Albany's transformation is convincing? What might have caused it?

Look at how Albany receives the news of Cornwall's death. How does this link in to Lear's view of the gods controlling men's lives?

Act 4, scene 3

◆ Kent meets the Gentleman again. He learns that Lear is near to the French camp but is too ashamed of his actions to confront his daughter.

Events 'off stage' are reported. Kent learns that the King of France had to return home to attend to urgent business, leaving Cordelia at Dover. The Gentleman describes Cordelia's tears when she read Kent's letter describing what had happened to her father. Lear has arrived at Dover but is so ashamed of how he treated Cordelia that he has not yet been able to face her.

Finally, we learn that the *powers* (armies) of both Cornwall and Albany are preparing for battle against the French.

Act 4, scene 4

◆ Cordelia sends soldiers to bring Lear into the camp. She expresses her love and concern for her father.

Cordelia learns that her father is nearby, wearing a crown of flowers, mad but not raging. She declares that her forces come not as foreign invaders, but to defend her father's rights. There can be a striking dramatic contrast in this scene when staged, between the soldiers and their battle camp and Cordelia's traditionally feminine 'gentle' virtues.

✪ What symbolic significance can be attached to Lear's wearing of a crown of flowers?

Act 4, scene 5

◆ Regan tries to discover the contents of a letter that Oswald is carrying from Goneril to Edmund. Regan sees her sister as a threat and reveals that she and Edmund have planned to marry.
◆ She tells Oswald there is a reward for killing Gloucester.

Oswald arrives at Gloucester's castle with the letter from Goneril for Edmund. (We must assume that several days have passed since Goneril and Edmund parted in Act 4, scene 2.) But Edmund is away on a *serious matter*. Regan tries to persuade Oswald to let her see the letter. Oswald refuses either to show the letter or stay at the castle even though Regan tries to detain him. Frustrated by Oswald's refusal, she tells him that she and Edmund have agreed to marry.

She admits it was a mistake to let Gloucester live, as the sight of the torture that was inflicted on him is turning many against their cause. She 'casually' mentions that there is a reward for the person who finds Gloucester and finishes him off. Unable to detain Oswald, she gives him something (a letter or gift) to take to Edmund.

Regan's private desires cloud her judgement. She hardly asks about the battle upon which her fate, and that of the kingdom, will depend, before quizzing Oswald about the letter he carries.

✪ Do we know anything of Edmund's feelings towards the sisters who are competing for his love at this point?

The balance of power is shifting again. The good characters are gathering at Dover, drawn to Cordelia as though she were a beacon of virtue (notice she never speaks in violent or vengeful terms), while the conspirators are both geographically scattered and pursuing conflicting ends.

❂ Look at Oswald's comment about Albany and Goneril, line 3. Why might he say this? How would you describe the true situation regarding Albany's and Goneril's capacity for fighting?

Act 4, scene 6

◆ Gloucester tries to throw himself from a cliff at Dover. Edgar uses deception to prevent his father from killing himself.
◆ Lear and Gloucester meet for the last time.
◆ Oswald tries to kill Gloucester to claim the reward but is himself killed by Edgar. As he lies dying, Oswald gives Edgar Goneril's letters to take to Edmund.
◆ Edgar reads in them that Goneril and Edmund are plotting against her husband Albany's life.

This long scene is best studied in three sections:

1 Gloucester's fall from the cliff and his 'miraculous' survival;
2 Lear's entry, his final phase of madness and the effect he has on those who see and hear him;
3 the fight between Edgar and Oswald.

Edgar leads Gloucester towards the cliffs at Dover. He goes through an elaborate pantomime of leading the blind man up a steep hill. He asks if he can hear the sea. Gloucester's hearing has grown acute since his blindness. He thinks Edgar's voice has changed from that he put on in the role of Poor Tom. Notice that Edgar is now described as being disguised as 'a peasant'. It is unclear whether he is still playing a version of Poor Tom or has changed into another role along the considerable journey on foot across England (about 150 miles if we assume Gloucester's castle was around Gloucester!).

But the problem of disguise is nothing compared to the difficulty of staging this strange mock-suicide scene. To modern eyes it can seem slightly absurd. Even a blind man crazed with grief might know if he had fallen from a huge cliff and miraculously survived or been duped into falling a couple of feet on a hillside. To make sense of how Shakespeare intended the scene to work we must think about theatre in his day. There were few props and no technical special effects, so Edgar has to draw the audience into sharing the fantasy he is weaving with the power of his words alone. Jacobean audiences were used to following and imagining a story without visual effects. They could probably 'listen' better than we can.

✪ How do you visualize the 'clifftop' scene? Note that it will help your memory of the play to visualize the key scenes in this way.

Look at the picture Edgar paints in lines 11–24. A good actor can transport the audience to that high cliff. When Gloucester makes his 'leap', his little jump, they will believe in the fantasy that Edgar has created. Edgar is on the side of good, and the audience will want his ruse to work, so they readily participate in it. None the less, there is a fine line here between tragedy and farce.

Likewise when Gloucester realizes he has miraculously survived, and Edgar rushes up and describes the amazing fall in another assumed voice, the audience will revel in the success of the deception, not laugh at what, to us, are the somewhat creaky and unlikely mechanics of it. A hint of eeriness is introduced when Edgar, now standing on the 'beach' with the fallen but living Gloucester, says the figure he thought he saw beside him on the summit was not a poor beggar but a demon. This would have been chilling to a Jacobean audience. (During performances of Marlowe's *Doctor Faustus*, a play about a man who sells his soul to the devil which was first performed at roughly the same time as Shakespeare was writing, audiences repeatedly claimed to see a real demon shadowing the actor playing the devil. Evil, for them, could easily take a demonic physical form.)

Edgar tries desperately to convince his father that the miracle occurred because the gods wanted to save him. But despite this, Gloucester remains suicidal.

Lear enters. Edgar is appalled to see the king is still mad, though it is a more whimsical and resigned insanity, almost free of rage. Gloucester recognizes Lear's voice, but Lear thinks Gloucester is Goneril with a beard and launches into a tirade against female sexuality. He is obsessed with female evil and cunning. He brings up Gloucester's past adultery.

❂ What is the irony in Lear's lines to Gloucester about Edmund: *kinder to his father/ Than were my daughters* (lines 115–16)?

Lear's journey to a painful but better understanding of the world is reaching its final stage. In his rant against social and sexual hypocrites (lines 160–73), Lear criticizes authority, including, presumably, kingly power, as being a sham. The rich escape justice because they bribe their way into the clear. Lear pities beggars who have no resources to cheat justice.

❂ What is the dramatic effect of putting true words about the evils of the world into the mouth of a madman? Why might Shakespeare have done this?

When Cordelia's search party arrives, Lear thinks they are trying to take him prisoner and he runs off. Gloucester seems to have been shaken out of his desire to die by seeing Lear. He thinks his own suffering is endurable if Lear can survive such madness.

The armies are drawn up ready to engage. Edgar still maintains to his father that he is *A most poor man ... pregnant to good pity* (lines 221–3). He is about to lead Gloucester to safety when Oswald appears. Oswald delightedly thinks he will kill Gloucester and earn the reward. Edgar, still disguised as a peasant, challenges him. ❂ Why is Oswald so ready to fight now, when he cried for help when attacked by Kent in Act 2?

Edgar fatally wounds Oswald, who, dying, asks Edgar to take the letters he carries, including Goneril's, to Edmund. One can at least say of Oswald that he is loyal to his mistress to his last breath.

Edgar reads the letters and discovers Goneril's plot against Albany's life to prepare the way for her union with Edmund. He decides to let Albany know of his wife's plans. Edgar leads his father to safety as a drum roll reminds us that battle looms.

Apart from Cordelia, whose return to pure feminine virtues rules her out as a warlike avenger, Albany, Edgar and Kent are the only major characters who can stand up for good in the resolution of the play, in the war between good and evil.

Albany has already stirred himself from his apathy in the vicious row with Goneril in Act 4, scene 2. Now Edgar is on the move. He has killed one of the (albeit minor) villains.

Act 4, scene 7

◆ Cordelia and Lear meet and are reconciled.

Lear has been caught and brought to Cordelia. She thanks Kent for his loyalty and good deeds. She urges him to put off his disguise but Kent claims he still needs its cover.

The weak, aged king is carried on stage in a chair. Compare this entry to the flourish that accompanied him in Act 1, scene 1. But everyone on stage defers to him: his kingship is recognized again. Lear wakes, but initially thinks he is in hell: *bound/ Upon a wheel of fire that mine own tears/ Do scald like molten lead* (lines 46–8). Then he recognizes his one true daughter and falls to his knees before her. He describes himself now not as a king but as *a very foolish, fond old man* (line 60). Cordelia says she feels no bitterness towards her father. As they leave to walk together Lear repeats this new humble view of himself:

> *You must bear with me*
> *Pray you now, forget and forgive: I am old and foolish.*
>   (lines 83–4)

Notice that Lear sees Goneril and Regan as the sole causes of his suffering. Though his manner is calm and humble, he does not see that his poor decisions may have caused all that has befallen him.

Before the battle

? Why do you think Edgar chooses not to reveal himself to his father during this Act?

? Regan's obsession with her own needs makes a strong contrast with Cordelia's generosity of spirit. Draw a Mini Mind Map detailing the differences, giving examples from any scene in the play.

? Given that Albany now is so clearly opposed to Goneril, Regan and Edmund, why do you think he is preparing forces to fight alongside Edmund against Cordelia's French army?

? Make a few clear notes comparing Cordelia's expression of love for her father in Act 4, scene 7, with her response to the love test in Act 1, scene 1.

Test your knowledge

Beside each of these quotes from Act 4 put (1) the name of the speaker, (2) to whom they are speaking, or what they are speaking about.

1 *The food of thy abused father's wrath!/ Might I but live to see thee in my touch ...*
2 *'Tis the time's plague when madmen lead the blind.*
3 *What most he should dislike seems pleasant to him.*
4 *'Twas he informed against him.*
5 *Something he left imperfect in the state/ Which since his coming forth is thought of ...*
6 *Her smiles and tears/ Were like a better way ...*
7 *Get thee glass eyes,/ And like a scurvy politician seem/ To see things thou dost not.*
8 *He's dead. I am only sorry/ He had no other deathsman.*
9 *... and in the mature time/ With this ungracious paper strike the sight/ Of the death-practised Duke.*
10 *O you kind gods,/ Cure this great breach in his abused nature!*

(Answers, see p. 91)

The play is reaching its climax. Take a break before Act 5.

Act 5, scene 1

◆ Regan challenges Edmund about his feelings for Goneril.
◆ Edgar gives Albany the letters revealing the plot against his life.
◆ Edmund vows to show Lear and Cordelia no mercy if he defeats the French army.

The battle is imminent. Edmund complains that his supposed ally Albany is full of indecision. Regan is convinced (line 5) that Oswald has been delayed or harmed. She asks Edmund if he is love with her sister. Again her private passions are threatening to interfere with strategy.

Albany and Goneril arrive. Seeing her sister alone with Edmund, Goneril declares *I had rather lose the battle than that sister/ Should loosen him and me* (lines 18–19). Albany and Edmund greet each other formally as allies, though Albany is at pains to point out immediately that he is on the battlefield because of the threat of a French invasion rather than to support the cause of Edmund and the sisters. The 'camp of evil' is turning against itself.

❂ What messages do you think Shakespeare is sending to the audience about the likely outcome of the battle? Given what actually happens, what dramatic tensions are being created?

Albany suggests (lines 31–2) that they consult experienced old soldiers on how to plan their attack. Edmund agrees to meet Albany at his tent.

Look at the exchange between the sisters, lines 34–7. Regan wants to keep Goneril in her sight while Edmund is about. Goneril's remark *O ho, I know the riddle, I will go* (line 37) indicates that she understands why Regan is trying to keep her in sight. They have effectively made their rivalry plain to one another. It is the start of their fatal personal conflict.

❂ The sisters are contributing to the ruin of their plans by fighting over a man. Do you think Shakespeare is following a tradition that portrays women as ruled by their private desires? Or is their rivalry a brilliant plot device? How does their behaviour in the last stages of the play contrast with that of the surviving male 'evil' character, Edmund?

Albany is about to leave the scene when Edgar, still disguised as a peasant, arrives. He gives Albany the letter he found on Oswald and tells him to open it before going into battle. He asks Albany to have a trumpet sounded if his army defeats the French. The fanfare will call forth a champion to prove the truth of the letter.

Edmund announces that the French are advancing. He gives another of his great speeches to the audience (lines 54—69). He has sworn his love to both sisters and cannot decide between them, but knows that *Neither can be enjoyed/ If both remain alive* (lines 57–8). ❂ What does he decide to do about this dilemma?

He knows that Goneril plans to murder Albany and seems quite happy to let this happen: apart from anything else it rids the stage of a man who might be a threat to his rise to power.

Edmund has been told that Albany intends to spare Lear and Cordelia if the French are defeated, but he plans to overrule Albany's clemency and have them killed. He ends this speech by saying his situation is too extreme for debate: he must defend, must act. It is a great statement of defiance before battle, clearly showing Edmund as the most powerful, and scheming, figure in the Albany–Goneril–Regan camp. He deals with three key issues in this short speech. Edmund is a man who thrives on plotting to achieve power. ❂ How would you describe Edmund's feelings for Goneril and Regan as revealed in this speech?

Act 5, scene 2

◆ The French are defeated.
◆ Edgar leads Gloucester away from the edge of the battlefield to safety.

We don't see the French lose the battle. Apart from the difficulty of staging battles, Shakespeare is less interested in the event than in the consequences. But notice the stage direction that opens this short scene that is effectively just a conversation between Edgar (still disguised as a peasant!) and Gloucester. Lear, Cordelia and French soldiers pass across the stage on the way to the battle. It is unlikely that Cordelia would be present at a battle, nor that she would have Lear beside her: the aim is more to show the forces of good in the play symbolically heading towards their doom.

 Gloucester refuses to be led any further by Edgar. He is overwhelmed by pessimism and thoughts of death. He has suffered enough. But finally he allows Edgar to lead him away from the danger of the lost battle.

This scene sets up the mood of pessimism that will hang like a storm cloud over the long last scene of the play.

Act 5, scene 3

- ◆ Edmund sends Lear and Cordelia off to prison and sends a death warrant after them.
- ◆ Albany accuses Edmund and Goneril of plotting against him.
- ◆ Regan feels unwell. Goneril, in an aside, reveals she has poisoned her sister.
- ◆ Albany arrests Edmund for treason.
- ◆ Albany has a trumpet sounded to call for a champion. Edgar appears, disguised in armour.
- ◆ Edgar fatally wounds Edmund in a duel.
- ◆ The dying Edmund confesses and regrets his actions. He reveals that the death warrant has been sent and urges Edgar to send to the prison to cancel it.
- ◆ News arrives that Goneril has killed herself.
- ◆ Lear enters carrying the body of Cordelia, who has been hanged. He dies of grief.

A huge scene of 325 lines, full of cruelty and anguish with barely a glimmer of hope for the future. There is darkness and violence. It is (along with the last scene of *Hamlet*) one of the bleakest and most bloody endings of any drama. The murder of Cordelia is the twist of the screw that can raise the drama to a pitch that can seem almost unbearable in a good stage production.

Edmund leads his prisoners onto the stage. Officers are ordered to take Lear and Cordelia to prison, but not before a much more settled and calm Lear describes (lines 8–19) how pleased he will be to suffer prison with his beloved and reconciled daughter. Away from the superficialities of court they *will sing like birds i' the cage* (line 9). They will outlast those in power, the *packs and sects of great ones/*

That ebb and flow by the moon (lines 18–19). Cordelia is distraught: we can imagine her in a stage production weeping quietly beside her father, who holds her protectively and now seems to be comforting her with such an optimistic view of prison life.

Lear's newfound authority and defiance, his caring for Cordelia and the eloquence of the poetry of the above speech, briefly lighten the gloom of the scene. Then Edmund, ever the reliable villain, brings down the mood of despair by sending a captain after the prisoners with a death warrant.

Edmund appears to be aspiring to the crown. But his place centre-stage is challenged by the arrival of Albany. After briefly praising Edmund's courage in the battle (and it is important to note that even Albany, who has true reason to hate Edmund, confirms that he is brave) he demands to see the prisoners. Edmund, anxious that the executions are carried out, plays for time, saying he will present them for trial in two or three days. But as ever in this play, the fine balances of power are moving again. Albany exerts sudden authority over Edmund, saying coldly:

I hold you but a subject of this war,
Not as a brother. (lines 61–2)

✪ Apart from knowing that Edmund is plotting with his wife behind his back, what other, more political, motives may Albany have for stressing to Edmund that he is a subject not an equal?

Regan and Goneril begin squabbling. Victory has not stopped their in-fighting. Regan declares her intention of marrying Edmund, but begins complaining of feeling unwell. Albany does not quite reveal that he knows about the plot against him hatched by Goneril and Edmund, but arrests Edmund for treason and indicates that Goneril is implicated.

As arranged with Edgar (in disguise) in Act 5, scene 1, Albany orders a trumpet to be sounded to call forth Edmund's accuser. He announces his own willingness to fight Edmund by throwing down his gauntlet as a sign of challenge. Shakespeare thus sets up in the audience's mind an understanding that Albany is physically brave, which we have not seen up to now.

Regan continues to complain of feeling unwell, while Edmund remains defiant despite being revealed as plotting with Goneril against Albany. He still has the blind courage or audacity of the absolute villain to throw down his glove, rising to the challenge against him, and to claim *What in the world he is/ That names me traitor, villain-like he lies* (lines 98–9).

 Regan is carried off to Albany's tent. At the third sounding of the trumpet Edgar appears 'armed'. This stage direction indicates that Edgar's identity is still hidden, probably by a helmet which covers his face. Theatre directors have used a variety of other means to mask Edgar's identity and to make his appearance at this point symbolic of avenging good. He may be masked, clad in heavy armour stripped from a dead soldier on the field, or otherwise dehumanized into a force able to challenge Edmund's still domineering energy.

They fight. Edmund is badly wounded. Goneril, in an act of gross hypocrisy, claims that the fight was unlawful. This goads Albany into presenting her with the letter she wrote to Edmund and which Edgar gave him. Like Edmund, Goneril won't step down in the face of growing evidence of guilt. She tries to snatch and destroy the letter before running off.

❂ What reason might Albany have for crying *Save him, save him!* (line 149) when Edmund falls?

Then something surprising happens. The dying Edmund confesses his crimes. If you have been rooting for, or at least rather guiltily admiring, the villain, this can be almost a disappointment! He says he will forgive his masked adversary if he is a nobleman. Remember the shock of Cornwall being stabbed by a servant: there is a parallel here in the suggestion that Edmund will not forgive his adversary if he is socially beneath him. Even in the face of death honour is important, which again is surprising given both Edmund's illegitimacy and actions.

Edgar reveals himself to Edmund. Edgar offers to *exchange charity* (line 164) but is unflinching in his condemnation of Edmund. Edmund accepts what Edgar says, *Thou'st spoken right, 'tis true;/ The wheel is come full circle, I am here* (lines 171–2). Edmund is referring to the Jacobean idea of the Wheel of Fortune. To Shakespeare's audience this would have been a recognized dynamic of drama. Villains climb up the wheel, gaining power, but at a crucial 'high point', their very energy and cunning propels them over the top of the circle and they begin their descent down the wheel to be crushed by it at the bottom. If Edmund is accepting that this is what has happened to him, he is accepting the sort of preordained powers he vigorously mocked in Act 1, scene 2.

Edgar and Albany embrace, signifying a possible positive future for the war-torn kingdom. Edgar describes his time as Poor Tom and Gloucester's guide, stressing his battle to keep Gloucester from despair. He regrets remaining in disguise for so long, but gives no reason for doing so.

Gloucester is dead. When Edgar finally revealed himself, the reunion was too much for the old man, who died of a broken heart, half grief-stricken, half joyful. A death caused by these contrasting emotions is a difficult concept to grasp during the flow of an event-packed play and there is a lull here, where Edgar mentions how Kent was affected by Gloucester's death.

The final, violent stage of the play commences when the Gentleman enters with a bloody knife and news that Goneril, knowing her game was up, has killed herself. Regan has died, poisoned by Goneril. Kent then arrives to say goodnight to his master, the king. Everyone realizes they have forgotten about Lear and Cordelia. This is a moment of great suspense, jolting everyone forward from the lengthy telling of stories and reports of actions off-stage that have been going on since the fight. Edmund *pants for life* (line 241) and as his death approaches admits he sent a death warrant to the prison. He urges the Gentleman to run to the prison and stop the executions. There is a moment of panic when Albany and Edmund work out how the prison will know it is Edmund who is ordering the stay of execution.

Edmund is carried off to die. As evil leaves the stage, good enters, in the form of Lear carrying the body of Cordelia. His madness has returned, but it is a despair caused by the death of the one daughter who truly loved him. Lear turns on the onlookers who stare aghast at what has happened. He calls them murderers and traitors for allowing his beloved daughter to die. We learn that he committed a final act of heroism for Cordelia: he killed the hangman (which is presumably why Lear is still alive). He begins to give up the will to live, his anguish is too great. Even the news that his tormentors, Goneril and Regan, are dead has no effect on the grief-stricken old man.

A good actor playing Lear invests his last moments on stage with a sense of distance. Lear is not really directly in touch with those around him; he is moving towards death, away from the suffering he has endured. To remain alive while Cordelia is dead would be agony. When Albany deals in state business, saying he will restore the kingdom to Lear and reinstate Kent and Edgar as earls, Lear hardly hears him. He is bent over the body of Cordelia.

Lear is a 'dead man walking', as Kent also feels himself to be. Kent was part of the old world, of Lear's reign, and like the dying king knows his time is past. He brushes aside Albany's suggestion that he share power with him if Lear dies. The kingdom is like a parcel that no one will accept.

✪ Do you think this is an unusual situation in a drama that deals with struggles for power? What effect might the idea that no one wants to take over the kingdom have had on an audience of Shakespeare's time? Write a few lines to explain your ideas.

As Lear dies, he thinks that perhaps Cordelia still lives. His last, rather enigmatic lines *Do you see this? Look on her: look her lips!/ Look there, look there!* (lines 308–9) suggest that he believes she is reviving.

Edgar believes Lear has only fainted. It is up to the stoical and realistic Kent to assure him that the king is dead and to sum up the situation:

> *Vex not his ghost; O, let him pass. He hates him*
> *That would upon the rack of this tough world*
> *Stretch him out longer.* (lines 311–13)

The king is dead. Kent thinks he will soon make a similar journey to the grave (lines 319–20). The anguish at the end of the play is unrelenting. Albany and Edgar, the younger generation, are left to take on the rule of the war-torn state, though finally Edgar alone is spoken of as the future ruler. He sums up the awful tragedy of the play by saying that though *The oldest have borne most; we that are young/ Shall never see so much, nor live so long.*

This final rhyming couplet suggests that the events they have been part of are so horrible that their lives will be blighted and shattered by them even though they suffered less than the old (Gloucester and Lear) who are dead. The good characters may have drawn together, but the damage wrought by the evil ones, especially Edmund, has left them with a world so tragic they find it hard to continue.

But life goes on!

? Many critics say that Cordelia's death is the cruellest moment in a cruel and bitter play. What if Lear had been executed first and Cordelia spared? What if both or neither of them had been killed? Make notes on how you think each of these endings might have worked and say why you think Shakespeare chose to end the play with Cordelia hanged and Lear dying of grief. Consider the dramatic effects of each option.

? Draw a Mini Mind Map to compare Lear's emotions as he dies with what we are told of Gloucester's last moments. List and briefly explain similarities and differences.

? Is anything in the ending of the play just? Write a short explanation of what acts of justice or fairness you think occur and what unfair things take place in this last Act. Is the overall feeling you get one of justice being done or of terrible unfairness?

Test your knowledge

Many of the themes we have identified feature in the climax of the play in Act 5. Answer these questions.

1. What creatures does Lear list as having life while his daughter Cordelia lies dead?

2. Who describes happiness in terms of singing birds?

3. Who *ebb and flow by the moon*?

4. What 'justice' requires *a fitter place* than the battlefield?

5. How do *three/ Now marry in an instant*, and where's the justice in this?

6. Paraphrase Edgar's comments in Act 5, scene 2, lines 9–11.

7. How do siblings turn against one another in Act 5?

8. What does Edgar ask of his father before the fight with Edmund?

9. Who is the *unknown opposite*?

10. Who put on *madman's rags* that *very dogs disdained*?

(Answers, see p. 91)

Answers to 'Test your knowledge'

ACT 1

1 Gloucester about Edmund.
2 Goneril to Lear.
3 Cordelia to Lear.
4 Cordelia about Burgundy.
5 Edmund to Gloucester about Edgar.
6 Goneril about Lear.
7 Lear about Oswald.
8 Lear cursing Goneril.
9 Goneril about Lear.
10 The Fool to Lear.

ACT 2

1 Edmund, pretending Edgar has wounded him.
2 Gloucester, searching for Edgar.
3 Until *noon*, but Regan extends the punishment to *all night too.*
4 In a hollow tree.
5 Lear.
6 Regan's.
7 Twenty-five.
8 *Basest beggars.*
9 The approaching storm.
10 *Not one.*

ACT 3

1 A ring.
2 Lear.
3 The rain!
4 Britain.
5 Edgar/Poor Tom.
6 A servingman.
7 *Little dogs.*
8 *Five- or six-and-thirty.*
9 Stabs him from behind.
10 Egg white.

ACT 4

1 Gloucester speaking about Edgar.
2 Gloucester speaking about Poor Tom/Edgar.
3 Oswald speaking about Albany.
4 Messenger speaking to Albany about Edmund's informing against Gloucester.
5 Gentleman speaking to Kent about the King of France's absence.
6 Gentleman speaking to Kent about Cordelia.
7 Lear speaking to Gloucester.
8 Edgar speaking about Oswald.
9 Edgar speaking to Gloucester about Albany.
10 Cordelia speaking about Lear.

ACT 5

1 *A dog, a horse, a rat.*
2 Lear.
3 *Great ones.*
4 The *question* of Cordelia and Lear.
5 Edmund, and Goneril and Regan (who both wanted to marry him), all die in the same scene. The main villains of the play have all come to nothing.
6 The process of being born is often painful: so is the process of dying. One must endure it until powers 'from above' intervene. A man should not wait until he is rotten, but die when ripe, or ready.
7 Goneril and Regan's army attacks Cordelia's, and Goneril poisons Regan.
8 His blessing.
9 Edgar.
10 Edgar.

CRITICAL APPROACHES

A huge number of critics have written about *King Lear*. The play has attracted a wide range of opinions and interpretations. It is considered by most Shakespeare scholars to be one of the greatest and most important of his plays. Most agree that it is a remarkable piece of work, a masterpiece. Some say it is so dense and complex that it should never be staged: the production will always fall short of the potential of the text. Some critics maintain that the play is one of the greatest works of literature in any form or culture.

Reading the opinions and arguments of critics is a very useful way of rounding out your own ideas about the play. But remember that whatever the critics have written, however well researched and intellectually rigorous, it is ultimately based on their own opinions and interpretations. And these are influenced by the thinking and beliefs in the society of their time. None of the critics whose ideas we will consider below ever spoke to Shakespeare!

Because so much has been written about *King Lear* we will review only the main areas of critical study.

The 'happy ending' (1681)

Most critics today would say that *King Lear* and *Hamlet* are the greatest of Shakespeare's tragedies. But while *Hamlet* has always been popular, *King Lear* dropped out of view for most of the seventeenth century after being first performed in 1606. *Macbeth* was more popular (and a lot shorter!).

Perhaps the bleakness of *King Lear* made it less appealing to audiences who wanted a tragedy where justice was done and there was a clearer way forward to a happier future. Perhaps because of this a writer called Nahum Tate produced a 'happy ending' version of the play in 1681 (less that seventy years after the 'real' Shakespeare version first appeared). Tate's version has Lear killing two soldiers sent to murder him and Cordelia in Act 5; then Edgar and Albany arrive to secure the safety of the king and his daughter. Edgar goes off to get his father, and the three old men (Lear, Gloucester and Kent) leave to enjoy a jolly sort of retirement together. Edgar marries Cordelia and they rule Britain.

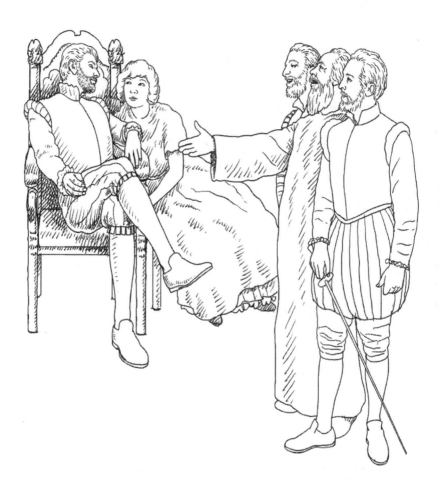

This version of the play was very popular on stage for over 150 years. It was revised by other theatre writers, including the famous actor/manager David Garrick. The 'happy ending' Lear was produced on stage until the mid-nineteenth century. Then theatre companies, scholars and critics began to look at the original text of what Shakespeare actually wrote (and remember there are two versions of the play; see pages 2–3). They found a work of towering genius but appalling bleakness. Today the Nahum Tate version is (thankfully!) never performed.

Pre-twentieth-century critics

Audiences in the eighteenth and nineteenth centuries were almost certainly more shocked than us by Shakespeare's bleak view of the world, and their critics reflected this. Some found Goneril and Regan too savage to be believed in, which is understandable when you consider how pre-twentieth-century society viewed women and the proper code of feminine behaviour.

Samuel Johnson accepted the successes that the sisters and Edmund enjoy (for a while at least) because he saw that this was a fair picture of how things often turned out in the real world. But even he found the ending of the play difficult: the awful injustice of Cordelia's death shocked him. It is worth noting, however, that even though these critics were influenced by the intellectual and moral climate of their times, they were picking up on elements in the play that concern some critics even today, in what we might think of as our more hard-bitten age.

Given that critics bring not only their personal preferences but also the mood of the society they live in to their reading of the play, it was perhaps inevitable that many early nineteenth-century and Victorian critics found *King Lear* too grim. Hazlitt said the play was dominated by *giddy anarchy*, but he thought Shakespeare showed a *firm faith in filial piety* in the character of Cordelia. Critics of this era struggled hard to find a Christian dimension to the play, even though it is set in pagan times. It is hard to sustain a belief in Christian virtues when so many times characters call on the gods but their appeals go unanswered. The debate between Christian and humanistic interpretations of the play continued into the twentieth century.

Twentieth-century critics

Much of the thinking and philosophy of the twentieth century has focused on the role and position of the individual and less on systems of belief and strict social order. This reflects a declining Christian intellectual climate and a growing humanistic one.

A. C. Bradley, an important early twentieth-century critic, believed the text would reveal its true meanings by close reading. He called the play *one of the world's greatest poems.* For him, it was fundamentally about characters and their motivation, as all Shakespearean tragedies are tragedies of an individual who suffers as he comes to terms with his own human character and failings.

In 1930 one of the most influential critical books on Shakespeare's works was published: G. Wilson Knight's *The Wheel of Fire.* In an essay called '*King Lear* and the Comedy of the Grotesque' he looked at an aspect of the play that had not been considered very much before. He does not use the word 'comedy' to mean comic in the usual humorous sense, but does identify a degree of 'comic' absurdity in some of the more vicious elements of the drama. This absurd violence makes the cruelty of the play more effective. Much of what happens is, according to Wilson, purposeless – violence for its own sake. He cites Lear's death, the king perhaps half crazed again; believing as he dies that Cordelia has started breathing and will live. In Wilson's reading of the play the gods torment man for no good reason but to cause them pain.

As we approach our own times we find critics less interested in debating whether or not the play contains a Christian dimension and more concerned with the political and social implications of the text. There have been studies written about the play analysing it in terms of gender (especially feminism), race, the family and politics.

In his book *Radical Tragedy*, J. Dollimore argues that Lear is less an individual than a product of the society in which he held a supreme position as king. Lear loses his mind not because of the suffering that his daughters call down upon him but because he has lost authority over his family and his kingdom. This is a subtle shift in position from what many people already thought about the character of Lear, but a crucial one because Dollimore emphasizes that Lear's madness is caused by a sudden and violent redistribution of power and property. He has shifted the emphasis from the human to the political. Just as the Christian critics of the previous century brought their principles to their study of the text, so Dollimore brings twentieth-century political thinking to his assessment of the play.

His reading of the play means it would have had a very strong subversive element to Jacobean audiences, for there are characters in it (Edmund especially) who almost manage to overthrow the established order of society and politics by sheer force of will. And Goneril and Regan successfully plot to force themselves into positions far beyond those which the society of Shakespeare's day generally allowed women to occupy. Although Edgar and Albany represent, as it were, a new generation of the old values, the world they inherit has been left shattered and perhaps irrevocably damaged by the actions of the characters who attempted to destroy the social and political *status quo*.

Late twentieth-century feminist critics have held contrasting opinions about the play. For some it is fundamentally about male anxiety. Lear goes mad when he realizes that he is dependent on his daughters. It is only when Lear admits to having a feminine side, symbolized by his finally being able to cry, that he recovers his sanity within a more equal and loving relationship with Cordelia. Interpreted in this way, Shakespeare can be seen to be exploring a feminist dynamic in the play.

But another feminist view asserts almost exactly the reverse and says that *King Lear* is horribly misogynistic and anti-feminine. Shakespeare, far from exploring the feminine potential in male characters, is presenting a drama that reinforces male prejudices towards women. Goneril and Regan embody all the hidden fears that (male) society has of women. They are portrayed as lustful and deceitful. They reject traditional submissive roles within the family structure and replace them with nothing but chaos that finally destroys them. The play focuses our sympathies totally onto male characters, principally Lear, Gloucester and Edgar. Cordelia has been wronged, but she is away in France married to a king and we never see her distress except when she meets Lear.

In 1999 American critic Harold Bloom put forward a radical new way of reading all Shakespeare's plays. A self-confessed 'Bardolitor' or Shakespeare-worshipper, he argues that the plays (especially *King Lear*) are not merely great because they so successfully portray complex human beings, but that the plays created what we now recognize as human personality. Before Shakespeare presented his vast cast of characters to the world, people had never been able to see the inner lives of real people. They had neither the vocabulary to talk about characters nor the insights to do so. Shakespeare created a world for each of his plays with characters whom the audience could study more deeply than they had ever studied actual people. Having seen the complexities of a character such as Lear, they were then able to see the humanity in people around them in a new and infinitely more enlightened way than previously. Shakespeare thus created in his dramas the basic understanding of what we call humanity.

This is a radical and daring view of the plays and elevates Shakespeare to an even higher status than before. You might like to think about how Bloom's view ties in with psychoanalysis, 'invented' at the start of the twentieth century, which has its own vocabulary and way of understanding how humans work. He certainly offers a totally new approach to the play.

Try this

? Mind Map the main critical approaches to the play. Add your own views.

Keep your critical faculties sharp: take a break.

Let's look closely at Act 4, scene 6, lines 106–74.

Read the passage very carefully. This is the only time in the play that Lear and Gloucester meet. A lot of information is conveyed in the conversation between the two most wronged characters. Both are at crucial points of change: Lear is still mad, but not raving as he was in the storm scene, and Gloucester, despite terrible suffering and grief, recognizes his old king.

Gloucester's identification of Lear by his voice underlines the slow returning to self and status that is just beginning to happen to Lear. Notice that Lear is beginning to speak in poetry again. But when Lear's madness surfaces and he rages at sexual licence (110–31) then against hypocrisy (161–73), he slips back from measured poetry to flowing prose, from the rhythmic language of the nobles to the speech of the poor and crazed.

Lear is returning in a confused way to seeing himself as, if not a king, then a figure of authority able to make judgements. His ironic amazement at the fact that anyone should die for committing adultery, and the rant against sexual licence, heavily tinged with revulsion, that follows it, should be acted on stage to show that he is posturing, feigning amazement. Lear sees sexual indulgence everywhere, in the natural world of *wrens* (birds) and flies.

His reference to Gloucester's *kinder* bastard son is probably not intended to cause the pain to Gloucester that it must do. But there is real pain in Lear's next line when he remembers the cruelty of his daughters who were *got 'tween lawful sheets*. This prick of pain launches Lear into his tirade against the posing and sexuality of women. His speech down to 129 is full of gross sexual allusions. The *simpering dame* has a *face between her forks* (between her legs), that *presages snow*: snow here suggesting coldness, chastity.

From 128 onwards Lear's speech becomes prose as his rage, and apparent madness, grow. He contrasts the 'tops' or visible characters of women, with their 'lower' halves, their sexuality.

He makes two contrasts of opposites to underline this duality: centaurs (mythical lustful creatures) and women, then gods and fiends. He invokes common images of hell to describe women's sexuality: *darkness ... sulphurous pit ... stench.* Although these are used symbolically, there is an unpleasant hint of physical description that shows the depth of Lear's venom towards women.

The last two lines of the speech see Lear suddenly calm. His madness is unpredictable. He asks an imaginary apothecary for a potion to calm his rage. Gloucester's reaction is that of a loyal courtier, tinged with great sorrow for his king. Lear won't let Gloucester kiss his hand because he thinks it smells of *mortality*, or death.

The series of exchanges between Lear and Gloucester based on images of eyesight and seeing (lines 132–50), reveal that while blind Gloucester has recognized his king, Lear may or may not know who Gloucester is. When Lear refers to Cupid it shows that his mind is still on relations between the sexes, but his thoughts have softened from sexuality to love. When Gloucester says he sees the world *feelingly,* by touch now that he is blind, Lear thinks he means feelingly in the sense of having great feeling for the world. This launches Lear into a further rage. But this speech, despite its racing images, has more method in the madness than his previous attack on women and female sexuality. Most readers and audiences would agree that there is a universal truth behind what he now says.

Lines 161–73 are a vivid and vicious attack on the hypocrisy that Lear has come to see as rampant in the world. His depth of outrage suggest that his anger at this situation may be contributing to his madness. Critics looking to place a Christian element in the play see this passage as being inspired by the Bible, Matthew 7:1–6, *Judge ye not, that ye be not judged.* In taking the side of the prostitute whipped by the *beadle* (parish officer), Lear echoes Jesus' pardoning of the adulterous woman.

Whether or not Shakespeare intended a Christian ethic to underlie this speech, it remains a great tirade against hypocrisy. The dramatic effect of putting such wise words into the mouth of a madman is to heighten their impact.

The beadle is a hypocrite because while he beats the prostitute he secretly lusts after her. The *usurer* (money lender) hangs the *cozener* (swindler): both are corrupt. The poor reveal their vices through their tattered clothes but the great and powerful can hide their sins under fine robes. *Furred gowns* suggests the robes worn by judges. The complex image of sin covered in gold or wealth being able to fend off the lance of justice whereas the rags of the poor are easily pierced, continues Lear's comparison of the different justice received by rich and poor. The poor always lose out. The king has had his view of the world transformed by his journey through madness. His view is now bitter, but clear.

But then he says none of this offends him, which appears contradictory. But Lear means that none, no one person offends him, because everyone does. He is playing the cynic when he says *I'll able 'em;/ Take that of me my friend* (lines 169–70). Lear is acting the king, giving sinners the right to continue their hypocritical sinning. (It is suggested that on stage Lear would hand a paper to Gloucester at this point, imitating the act of passing over a royal order or consent.)

Lear closes his speech by returning to the theme of blindness, advising Gloucester to get *glass eyes* with which he will see, *like a scurvy politician,* or shabby schemer, the true nature of the world. Glass eyes could have two meanings. Lear could be referring to false eyes, which would not help Gloucester see at all, or spectacles, which could, symbolically if not actually, aid seeing.

The passage ends with another utterance that is confused for lack of a stage direction and needs to be seen accompanied by action on stage. When Lear says *Now, now, now, now,/ Pull off my boots, harder, harder, so,* he could be consoling Gloucester, who is weeping at the state of his king, while tugging at real or imaginary boots. Or, in his distracted state, Lear could be ignoring Gloucester, the kingly audience having come to a close in his scattered mind, and be concentrating on his footwear. Acting out the close of speech makes the meaning clear either way with appropriate actions.

HOW TO GET AN 'A' IN ENGLISH LITERATURE

In all your study, in coursework, and in exams, be aware of the following:

- **Characterization** – the characters and how we know about them (e.g. speech, actions, author description), their relationships, and how they develop.
- **Plot and structure** – story and how it is organized into parts or episodes.
- **Setting and atmosphere** – the changing physical scene and how it reflects the story (e.g. storm reflecting chaos).
- **Style and language** – the author's choice of words, and literary devices such as imagery, and how these reflect the mood.
- **Viewpoint** – how the story is told (e.g. through an imaginary narrator, or in the third person but through the eyes of one character – 'She was furious – how dare he!').
- **Social and historical context** – the author's influences (see 'Context').
- **Critical approaches** – different ways in which the text has been, or could be, interpreted.

Develop your ability to:

- Relate **detail** to **broader content, meaning and style**.
- Show understanding of the author's **intentions, technique and meaning** (brief and appropriate comparisons with other works by the same author will gain marks).
- Give **personal response and interpretation**, backed up by **examples** and short **quotations**.
- **Evaluate** the author's achievement (how far does the author succeed – give reasons).

Make sure you:

- Use **paragraphs** and **sentences** correctly.
- Write in an appropriate **register** – formal but not stilted.
- Use short appropriate quotations as **evidence** of your understanding.
- Use **literary terms** correctly to explain how an author achieves effects.

THE EXAM ESSAY

Planning

You will probably have about 45 minutes for one essay. It is worth spending 5–10 minutes planning it. An excellent way to do this is in the three stages below.

1 **Mind Map** your ideas, without worrying about their order yet.
2 **Order** the relevant ideas (the ones that really relate to the question) by numbering them in the order in which you will write the essay.
3 **Gather** your evidence and short quotes.

You could remember this as the **MOG** technique.

Writing and checking

Then write the essay, allowing five minutes at the end for checking relevance, spelling, grammar and punctuation.

Remember!

Stick to the question, and always **back up** your points with evidence in the form of examples and short quotations. Note: you can use '. . .' for unimportant words missed out in a quotation.

Model answer and plan

The next (and final) chapter consists of an answer to an exam question on *King Lear*, with the Mind Map and plan used to write it. Don't be put off if you think you couldn't write an essay like this yet. You'll develop your skills if you work at them. Even if you're reading this the night before the exam, you can easily memorize the MOG technique in order to do your personal best.

The model answer and plan are good examples to follow, but don't learn them by heart. It's better to pay close attention to the wording of the question you choose to answer, and allow Mind Mapping to help you to think creatively and structurally.

Before reading the answer, you might like to do a plan of your own to compare with the example. The numbered points, with comments at the end, show why it's a good answer.

M ODEL ANSWER AND ESSAY PLAN

QUESTION

Read Act 1, scene 4, from line 185 through to 286 (from Goneril's entrance to Lear's exit). Discuss how this scene develops our knowledge of the characters and moves the plot forward.

NOTE

Elements for a model answer. This question asks you to look closely at one section of a long scene. You need to refer to links with other parts of the play, but your focus should be on what happens in the 101 lines of the selected section.

The passage is a key moment in the development of the main plot involving Lear and his daughters. You will find that making a Mind Map of the main elements you need to include in your answer will help you focus on the important points and stop you getting side-tracked into considering things that are not actually part of the structure and content of this scene. Make the Mind Map before you begin writing the essay.

Your Mind Map should look something like the one on p. 104.

PLAN

1 Context.
2 Motives.
3 Relationships.
4 Staging.
5 Interpretation.
6 Quotes.
7 Close reading.
8 Conclusion.

26128

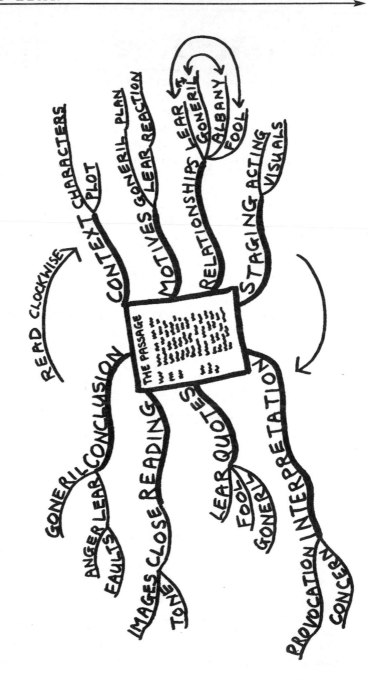

ESSAY

Lear is staying at Goneril's castle. His visit is the first (we assume) of his proposed cycle of stops with her and Regan in turn. He is travelling with one hundred knights to keep up the appearance of being a king. We have already heard, at the end of Act 1, scene 1, Goneril and Regan discussing how they need to be careful about the new arrangement of power in the kingdom. Goneril took the lead there suggesting that they 'must do something, and i' the heat' (line 306).[1]

In Act 1, scene 3, we hear Goneril talking to her steward, Oswald, about Lear's visit. She complains of the rowdiness of his train of knights and encourages Oswald to be less than respectful to the king. We know that Lear has a temper and this is a sure way of provoking him. Goneril has set the stage for a confrontation with Lear. The passage we are directed to in this question shows us Lear's reaction.[2]

There are four characters to consider: Lear, Goneril, the Fool and Albany. How they relate to one another creates the dramatic conflict of the passage. There are three relationships interweaving through the passage:

1 What is said by Lear and Goneril to one another is the most important element of the scene. This is the first time we see Goneril implementing her plan to reduce Lear's power. It is the first time we see Lear reacting to this sudden disrespect from his daughter.

2 The Fool's comments to, or often at, Lear, show us the development of the relationship between him and his master, the king. The relationship between the Fool and Goneril is much less important and is hardly touched on. Notice that the Fool speaks in prose because he is a common man. The others, the nobles, speak in poetry.

3 Albany has only a few lines at the end of the passage. They reveal something of the relationship between himself and his wife, and of his rather weak character at this point in the play. His attitude towards Lear is no more than would be expected of a nobleman towards a king. He does not speak to his wife.[3]

It is important to consider how this scene could be played on stage. This is primarily a scene of words. There are no significant actions. Its drama is in the conflict between the characters. They are all involved in some conflict: Lear and

Goneril with one another, the Fool with Lear, Albany with the situation he arrives into and cannot understand. But up to line 269 there are knights and attendants around the scene, so Lear and Goneril are speaking in public. This might affect what they feel able to say. On stage the scene would have its own audience of Lear's knights. Their presence contributes to the tension between Lear and Goneril because Lear's authority is being publicly challenged. Note that apart from the exits of Kent and the Knight, and Albany's arrival, there are no stage directions in the passage.[4]

The passage starts where Goneril enters. We do not know if she is really angry, if Lear's knights are behaving in a way that upsets her. She could be pretending to be offended in order to provoke an argument with Lear. But we must remember that we have been given two clear indications already that the sisters, led by Goneril, are plotting against Lear, so Goneril should be seen as acting the injured party here. This adds to the dramatic conflict of the scene. If her complaints were justified, the row with Lear would have little dramatic purpose.[5]

The Fool may be more aware of things developing than his master. He ignores Goneril's arrival and begins one of his many taunts against Lear. The recurring theme and imagery of nothingness comes up here when he says to Lear, 'I am better than thou art now. I am a fool, thou art nothing' (lines 188–9). A few lines later he echoes this by calling Lear 'a shelled peascod', an empty husk.[6]

Goneril's first long speech to Lear in this passage (lines 196–209) lays out her complaints (genuine or contrived) about Lear's attendants, including the 'all-licenced fool' who has just spoken. It is phrased in icy good manners: note how she calls Lear 'Sir' in line 199.

This speech could be taken in two ways. Most obviously and probably, Goneril is using the knights as an excuse to begin her attack on Lear's position. But her complaints could be taken as reasonable, and if we consider that she is now queen of half of England then being seen to have such a rowdy house could harm her image and position. But again the Fool seems to see how things lie more quickly than Lear when, after Goneril has finished, he tells Lear his little story of the mother bird who had its head eaten by its ravenous young.

Lear is stunned by Goneril's complaints. The issue of identity (a recurring theme in the play) is raised twice. Lear is so amazed by Goneril's changed attitude to him that he first says, 'Are you our daughter?' (line 214). Note the use of the royal plural, 'our' not 'my': Lear still regards himself as a king. When she stands fast he questions his own identity: surely he must be changed into someone else to be spoken to like this? Lear is speaking with bitter irony here, he is not yet so distressed that he is actually questioning his own identity. His questions are rhetorical, not meant to be answered, but when he concludes his self-questioning, 'Who is it can tell me who I am?' (line 226), quick as a flash the Fool sticks another barb in by answering 'Lear's shadow'.[7]

Notice also that Lear refuses to hear any criticism of his followers. This could be sheer arrogance. It could also reveal a better side to Lear's nature (that we have seen in his hiring of Kent disguised as a plain serving man): that he is fiercely loyal and protective of those who are loyal to him.

Goneril's next long speech (lines 233–47) again can be read as a reasonable description of a problem and a request that Lear reduce his train of attendants to solve it. It builds up the case she has already laid out. If we did not know her 'hidden agenda' we might think this a perfectly reasonable argument. But Lear's response is to fly into a rage and threaten to leave. He calls Goneril a 'Degenerate bastard'. Lear's temper, which we have already seen when he disinherited Cordelia, is causing him to react rashly.

Albany hears Lear's shouts, and enters. He has very little to say beyond urging calm. Lear ignores him, calling Goneril a 'Detested kite' (line 259), an instance of the animal imagery that occurs throughout the play, often to describe Goneril. Lear refuses to hear any criticism of his knights. He orders his attendants, including Kent, out, still making as if to leave. This makes a dramatic difference to the scene on stage and creates a more private arena for the final stages of the conflict between Lear and his daughter. Albany only really hovers around the edge of their dispute.[8]

Lear's parting is a vicious attack on his daughter. Goneril is cursed because she is acting unnaturally in challenging her father's wishes. In return, Lear acts equally unnaturally in launching such a sustained verbal attack. He hopes she will be sterile and never have children, or if she does that they hate and destroy her. Then she will feel how painful ('sharper than a serpent's tooth' – another animal image) 'it is to have a thankless child'.[9]

We can see how power has shifted in this scene. Lear has been challenged, and by leaving Goneril's house, as he eventually does as a direct result of her complaint, he is effectively retreating. He has shouted and raved, but Goneril has won by being quiet and firm. The contrast between their speeches creates much of the dramatic effect of the scene. Goneril orders her complaints rationally and with very little addition of images: Lear uses much more imaginative language and imagery to vent his anger.[10]

WHAT EARNED THE MARKS?

1 The introduction locates the passage in the unfolding drama.
2 The second paragraph explains the intentions behind the actions of the passage.
3 This analysis of relationships shows a grasp of the structure of the passage.
4 The view of the staging shows awareness that the play is written for performance.
5 Shows an understanding of alternative interpretations of the text.
6 Quotes used to show the theme of nothingness and the imagery Shakespeare uses to convey it.
7 Close reading of the text is shown here.
8 Shows awareness of how the piece gains extra meaning when performed.
9 It is too easy to see Lear as a victim throughout the play. Here the writer shows that he has faults, a flawed personality that contributes to bringing down misfortune on his own head.
10 Summing up shows understanding of the implications of what has happened.

GLOSSARY OF LITERARY TERMS

alliteration   the repetition, for effect, of consonant sounds.

allusion   the use of literary, cultural and historical references.

assonance   the repetition, for effect, of vowel sounds.

caricature   exaggeration and simplification of character traits.

characterization   the way in which characters are presented.

context   the background of social, historical and literary influences on a work.

dialect   regional form of language varying from the standard in vocabulary and grammar.

diction   choice and arrangement of words.

didactic   intended to instruct; in literary criticism, often used in negative sense.

discursive   presenting a logical argument, step by step.

feminist criticism   critical approach developed in the 1960s, based on assessing the role of gender in texts. A particular issue is the subordination of women in a patriarchal society.

genre   type of literary work conforming to certain expectations; e.g. tragedy.

groundlings   members of the Elizabethan and Jacobean theatre audience who stood in the pit or floor area in front of the stage. (Also known as 'stinkards'!)

humanistic   philosophy centring on human ends and conditions, rather than, say, religious.

iambic   two-syllable 'foot' or unit of poetry, consisting of an unstressed syllable followed by a stressed one. (See also *pentameter*.)

idiom   a characteristic expression of a language or *dialect*.

image   a word picture bringing an idea to life by appealing to the senses.

irony   a style of writing in which one thing is said and another is meant, used for a variety of effects, such as criticism or ridicule.

Marxist criticism   critical approach which sees literature in relation to class struggle, and assesses the way texts present social realities.

metaphor   a compressed *simile* describing something as if it were something else.

parody   an exaggerated copy (especially of a writer's style) made for humorous effect.

pentameter   a line of poetry consisting of ten syllables. The iambic pentameter (see *iambic*) is the standard line of poetry used by Shakespeare in his plays.

persona   an assumed identity.

personification   an *image* speaking of something abstract, such as love, death or sleep, as if it were a person or a god.

plot   the story; the events that take place and how they are arranged.

polemical   (of style) making an argument.

rhetorical   expressed with a view to persuade (often used in negative sense)

satire   literature which humorously exposes and ridicules vice and folly.

simile   an *image* comparing two things similar in some way but different in others, normally using 'like' or 'as'.

structure   the organization of a text; e.g. narrative, plot, repeated images and symbols.

subplot   subsidiary plot coinciding with the main plot and often reflecting aspects of it.

tone   the mood created by a writer's choice and organization of words; e.g. persuasive.

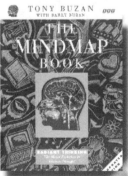